Eyes Open 2

COMBO A

STUDENT'S BOOK

Ben Goldstein & **Ceri Jones**
with **Emma Heyderman**

Starter Unit

Family

1 🔊 1.01 **Listen and complete Nathan's family tree with the names in the box.**

Sophie Dave Ben Henry Anne
Tom Phil Diana Marie Lucy

2 **Complete the table with the words in the box.**

~~parents~~ ~~mum~~ ~~brother~~ husband dad
aunt sister grandma cousin uncle
wife granddad grandparents

mum,	brother,	parents,
♀	♂	♀♂

Subject pronouns and *be*

3 **Complete the examples from the listening in Exercise 1.**

	I	you / we / they	he / she / it
+	**I** [1] *'m* Nathan.	**You're** 13.	**He** [2] .... from Newcastle.
–	**I'm not** Matthew.	**You aren't** 12.	My dad [3] .... from Liverpool.
?	**Am I** right?	**Are you** from Scotland?	[4] .... your family big?

➔ **Grammar reference • page 98**

4 **Complete the questions with the correct form of *be*. Then complete the answers with the correct subject pronoun.**

1 Where *'s* your mum from?
She's from Barcelona.
2 What .... your dad's name? ....'s Pete.
3 .... you in a sports team?
Yes, ... am. ....'m in the basketball team.
4 How old .... your granddad? ....'s 82.
5 .... your parents teachers? No, ... aren't.

Possessive *'s*

5 **Look at the examples from the listening in Exercise 1 and put the apostrophe (') in the correct place.**

1 My mums name is Marie.
2 My grandparents names are Henry and Diana.

➔ **Grammar reference • page 98**

Your turn

6 **Write questions with the correct form of *be* and possessive *'s*. Use one word from each box. Then ask and answer the questions with your partner.**

Where What Who When	parents classmates cousin best friend	favourite singer favourite book birthday English lesson

When's your mum's birthday?

It's on 20 May.

School subjects

1 Complete the school subjects. Then match them with the pictures.

1 Fr _ nch
2 _ ngl _ sh
3 M _ s _ c
4 Sc _ enc _
5 _ CT
6 P _
7 G _ _ gr _ phy
8 M _ ths
9 H _ st _ ry

a 

b 

c 

d 

e 

f 

g 

h 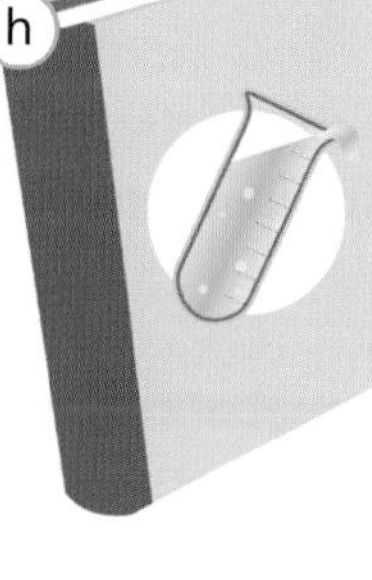

i 

2 1.02 **Listen to Nathan talking to his cousin Lucy about his school. Which of the school subjects in Exercise 1 do you hear?**

there is/are and *some* and *any*

3 Complete the examples from the listening in Exercise 2. When do we use *some* and *any*?

	Singular	Plural
+	**There** [1].... **some** cola in the fridge.	**There** [3].... **some** classrooms in the main building.
–	**There isn't any** orange juice.	**There** [4].... **any** laptops in our classroom.
?	[2].... **there any** orange juice?	[5].... **there any** science labs at your school?

Grammar reference • page 98

4 Write sentences with *there is/are* and *some/any* about the things and places in your school in the box below.

~~posters~~ food computers balls laptops students science lab ~~classroom walls~~ library IT room canteen sports hall

There are some posters on the classroom walls.

have got + a/an

5 Complete the examples from the listening in Exercise 2.

	I / you / we / they	he / she / it
+	I [1].... PE tomorrow.	My school's [4].... four labs.
–	We [2].... **got an** IT room.	It **hasn't got** any laptops.
?	**Have** you [3].... **a** big sports hall?	**Has** Lucy **got a** laptop?

Grammar reference • page 99

Your turn

6 Write questions with *have got*. Use the people and the things below. Then ask and answer your questions with a partner.

you your best friend your mum, etc. your teacher your classmates	Maths, History, PE, etc. a big family a mountain bike a laptop an English dictionary

Have you got PE today?

Yes, I have.

Sports and activities

1 Match the pictures with the sports in the box.

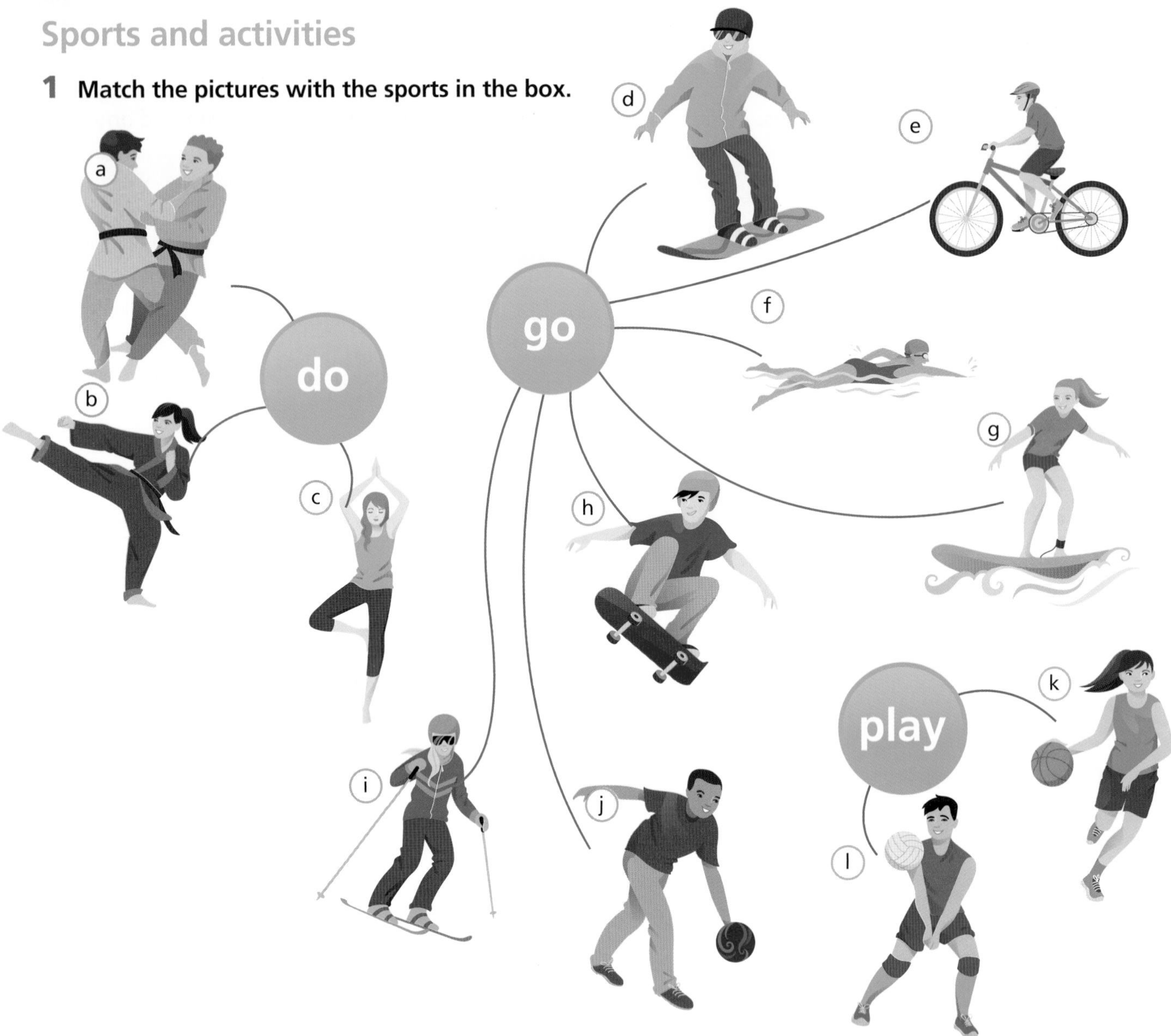

judo volleyball bowling skiing swimming snowboarding cycling skateboarding basketball surfing karate yoga

2 1.03 Listen to Nathan and Lucy talking about their free time. Which of the sports and activities in Exercise 1 does Nathan do? Which of them does Lucy do?

Present simple: affirmative and negative

3 Complete the examples from the listening in Exercise 2.

	I / you / we / they	he / she / it
+	I [1] *like* surfing My friends and I usually [3] .... cycling.	He sometimes [2] .... bowling with granddad.
–	You **don't** [4] .... near the sea.	He [5] .... **like** it very much.

Grammar reference • page 99

4 Complete the sentences with the present simple form of the verb in brackets.

1 I .... (go) snowboarding with my parents in the winter.
2 My friends .... (have) football training on Fridays.
3 I .... (not play) volleyball very often.
4 My sister .... (do) drama after school.
5 My uncle .... (not play) chess.
6 My friends and I .... (ride) our bikes to school every day.
7 We .... (not live) near the sea so I .... (not go) surfing.

5 Rewrite the sentences in Exercise 4 so they are true for you.

1 *I don't go snowboarding with my parents in the winter. We don't live near the mountains.*

Present simple: questions

1 Complete the examples from the listening on page 6.

	I / you / we / they	he / she / it
Wh-?	What sports [1]*do* you **do**? When **do** they **go** bowling?	How often **does** he **go** snowboarding?
Y/N?	[2].... you **go** swimming?	[3].... your sister **go** surfing too?
Short answers	Yes, I **do**. No, I [4].... .	Yes, she [5].... . No, he **doesn't**.

Grammar reference • page 99

2 Write questions about your sentences in Exercise 5 on page 6.

1 When / you / go snowboarding?
When do you go snowboarding?
2 When / your friends / have training?
3 you / play volleyball?
4 your sister / do drama after school?
5 What sports and activities / your uncle / do?
6 How / you and your friends / go to school?
7 you / go surfing?

Your turn

3 Work with a partner. Ask and answer your questions in Exercise 2.

When do you go snowboarding?

I don't go snowboarding with my parents in the winter. We don't live near the mountains. What about you?

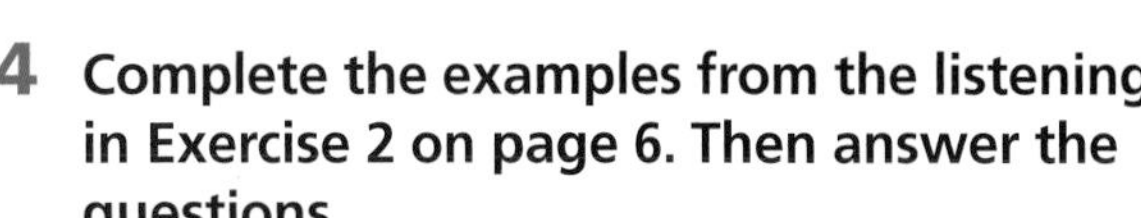

Adverbs of frequency

4 Complete the examples from the listening in Exercise 2 on page 6. Then answer the questions.

1 My friends and I .... go cycling on Saturday afternoons.
2 I .... go swimming with Mum and Dad.
3 The water's .... cold.
4 He .... goes now.

1 Does the abverb of frequency go before or after the verb *be*?
2 Does the adverb of frequency go before or after other verbs?

Grammar reference • page 99

5 Rewrite the sentences with the adverbs of frequency in the correct place.

1 We do ICT in the IT room. (usually)
We usually do ICT in the IT room.
2 My friends play basketball at school. (sometimes)
3 I do yoga at school. (never)
4 My grandparents go bowling. (sometimes)
5 My cousin does judo at the weekend. (often)
6 I go cycling on Sunday morning. (always)

Your turn

6 Write true sentences about you. Use the present simple, adverbs of frequency and the words below.

- have lunch in the school canteen
- be tired on Monday morning
- play basketball in the sports hall
- go bowling
- go swimming in the sea
- do Science in the science lab

I always have lunch in the school canteen.

7 Work with a partner. Use '*How often...?*' and the present simple to ask and answer questions about your sentences in Exercise 6.

How often do you have lunch in the school canteen?

I always have lunch in the school canteen.

1 Money matters

Discovery EDUCATION

In this unit ...

Unusual fun **p11**

Tiger sanctuary **p14**

Shopping **p16**

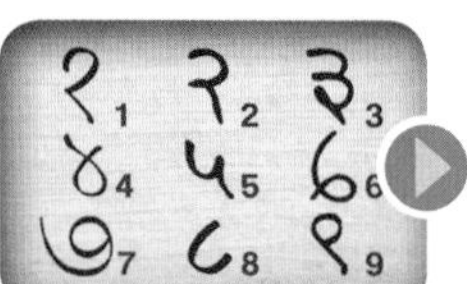

CLIL What does Zero mean? **p116**

Vocabulary
- Shops
- Money verbs
- Extreme adjectives
- Adjective prefixes

Language focus
- Present continuous
- Present simple vs. continuous
- *would prefer to, would(n't) like to, don't want to*
- *enough*

Unit aims
I can ...
- talk about shops and shopping centres.
- talk about the things I'm doing now and the things I do every day.
- understand a conversation about how young people spend their money.
- describe things I want to, would like to or would prefer to do.
- understand information about charities.
- ask for things in shops.
- write an email asking for advice.

BE CURIOUS

What can you see in the photo?
Start thinking
- **What can you buy at this market?**
- **Where do you think it is?**
- **Where do you buy things in your town?**

Vocabulary Shops

1 1.04 **Match the pictures with the words in the box. Then listen, check and repeat.**

bookshop chemist clothes shop department store electronics shop music shop newsagent shoe shop sports shop supermarket

2 Look at Exercise 1.

Which places sell …

1 food and drink?
2 things to read?
3 things to wear?

Where can you …

4 buy a new computer?
5 listen to music?
6 go when you feel ill?

Your turn

3 Write your answers to the questions.

1 What kind of shops do you like?
2 When do you go there?
3 Who do you go with?
4 What do you buy there?

My favourite shop is a music shop. I go there on Saturday with my friends.

4 Work with a partner. Ask and answer the questions in Exercise 3.

Vocabulary bank • page 108

Reading A blog

1 **Look at the photos of a shopping centre in Dubai. What can you do there?**

2 1.05 **Read Liam's blog and check your ideas to Exercise 1. Then match the photos to the places in bold.**

a *Sega Republic*

3 **Read Liam's blog again. What are the numbers about?**

1200	22	120	50 million	150

Explore extreme adjectives

4 **Look at the adjectives from Liam's blog. Do they mean very good or very bad?**

great awful wonderful brilliant amazing

5 **Find three adjectives in the text that mean *very hot*, *very cold* and *very big*. Do we use *very* or *absolutely* before these adjectives?**

Vocabulary bank • page 108

Your turn

6 **Work with a partner. Ask and answer the questions.**

1 Would you like to visit the Dubai Mall?
2 What would you like to do there?
3 Are there many shopping centres in your town?
4 How often do you go there?
5 What other things can you do there?

HOME < OLDER POSTS SUBSCRIBE

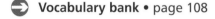

Dubai

AN ENGLISH BOY IN DUBAI

I'm Liam. I'm 15 years old and I'm from Cambridge. My parents are working in Dubai this year so I'm writing all my news about life here on this blog. Hope you like it!

A DAY AT THE MALL

POSTED BY ENGLISHBOYINDUBAI
SATURDAY 20 APRIL

Today I'm spending the day in Dubai Mall with my family. It's great! It's got about 1,200 shops, 22 cinema screens and 120 cafés and restaurants.

More than 50 million people visit the mall every year because there are a lot of cool things to do here. Luckily, there aren't only shops because I hate shopping. It's awful! My dad and my sister are watching the fish right now in the wonderful **Underwater Zoo**. There are more than 33,000 fish there – even sharks!

Outside it's boiling so why am I wearing a sweater? Because I'm skating on the **Olympic-size ice rink** and it's absolutely freezing. The temperature of the ice is below zero! After the ice rink, I want to go to the mall's theme park, the **Sega Republic**. It's brilliant – it's got 150 games and rides.

And what are my mum and aunt doing? They're looking at the **Dancing Fountain**. It's 152 metres high! At night, there's an amazing light show. On a clear night, you can see it from space!

a

b

c

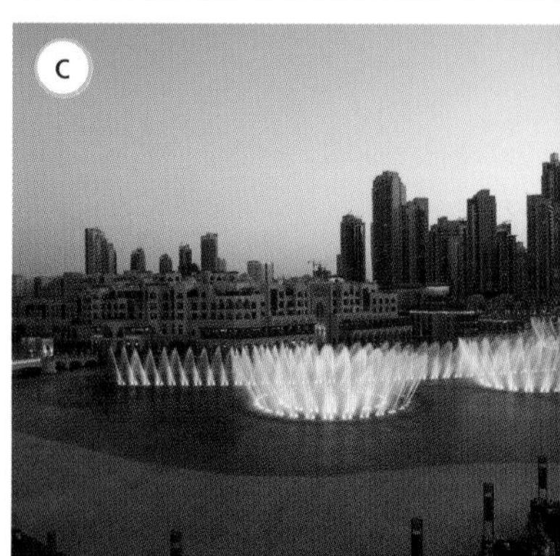

FACT! *The Dubai Mall is absolutely huge! It's the size of 50 football pitches. It's the biggest shopping centre in the world!*

d

Language focus 1 Present continuous

1 **Complete the examples from the text on page 10.**

	I	he / she / it	you / we / they
+	I [1]…. **spending** the day in Dubai Mall.	My friend **is shopping**.	My dad and my sister **are** [2]…. the fish.
–	**I'm not going** to the zoo.	Liam's mum **isn't shopping**.	Liam's dad and sister **aren't skating**.
?	Why [3]…. I **wearing** a sweater?	**Is** Liam **wearing** a sweater?	What **are** my mum and aunt [4]…. ?

Grammar reference • page 100

Get it right!

Spelling the *-ing* form:
For verbs ending in -e, remove the e: *write* → ***writing***
For verbs ending with one vowel and one consonant, double the final consonant: *shop* → ***shopping***

2 **Write sentences in the present continuous with the verbs in brackets.**

1 They …. (write) text messages on their phones.
They're writing text messages on their phones.
2 He …. (not listen) to the teacher!
3 I …. (make) a cake for my brother's birthday.
4 We …. (not watch) TV. There's nothing to watch!
5 Nicky …. (run) in the park today.

3 **Write questions in the present continuous. Then answer them for you.**

1 What / your teacher / do?
What is your teacher doing? She's writing on the board.
2 Where / you / sit / now?
3 Why / you / learn English?
4 you / listen to music / at the moment?
5 your friends / play football / now?

Present simple vs. continuous

4 **Read the sentences from Liam's blog and answer the questions. Then complete the rule with *simple* or *continuous*.**

a Today **I'm spending** the day in Dubai Mall.
b More than 50 million people **visit** the mall every year.

1 Which sentence talks about an action in progress?
2 Which sentence talks about a fact, habit or routine?

We use the **present** [3]…. to talk about facts, habits and routines and the **present** [4]…. to talk about an action in progress.

Grammar reference • page 100

Your turn

5 **Complete the questions with the present simple or present continuous form of the verb in brackets.**

1 What …. you …. (do) now?
2 What do you think your parents …. (do) now?
3 What …. you usually …. (do) at the weekend?
4 Where …. you usually …. (go) after school?
5 What …. your classmates …. (do) now?
6 Where …. you usually …. (go) on holiday?
7 …. you …. (read) a good book at the moment?

6 **Work with a partner. Ask and answer the questions in Exercise 5.**

What are you doing now?

I'm talking to you in my English class!

Learn about having fun in Dubai.

- Where are the young people snowboarding outdoors?
- Where are they snowboarding indoors?
- What shop do the young people like visiting?

1.1 Unusual fun

Listening A radio programme

1 Look at the photos. Which things have you got?

2 1.06 Listen to a radio programme. Which of the things in Exercise 1 have Josh and Megan got in their bags?

3 1.06 Listen again and choose the correct answers.

1 Josh wants to buy **a games console / a mobile phone**.
2 Josh is shopping with **his pocket money / his birthday money**.
3 Josh and his family **buy / don't buy** clothes online.
4 Josh is shopping with **his family / his friends**.
5 Megan **gets / doesn't get** pocket money.
6 Megan **likes / doesn't like** getting money for her birthday.

Vocabulary Money verbs

4 1.07 Look at the pictures and complete the sentences with the present continuous form of the verbs in the box. Then listen, check and repeat.

earn	sell	borrow	buy	save	spend

1 He .... his bike.

4 He .... all his money on some new trainers.

2 He .... money in a jar.

5 He .... money washing his dad's car.

3 He .... a book.

6 He .... money from his brother.

5 Choose the correct words.

1 I never **sell / buy / borrow** clothes online. I like to try them on first.
2 I don't save my money. I usually **spend / buy / borrow** it all at once.
3 I'm **earning / spending / saving** for a new mobile phone.
4 I want to **buy / sell / borrow** my old bike. I've got a new one now.
5 I sometimes **save / earn / spend** money by cleaning my dad's car. He gives me £2.
6 I often **borrow / save / sell** money from my sister when I want to buy something.

Your turn

6 Rewrite the sentences in Exercise 5 so they are true for you.

1 *I often buy clothes online but I sometimes try them on first.*

7 Ask and answer questions with the verbs in Exercise 4. Use these question beginnings.

- How often do you …?
- Are you …ing at the moment?
- Do you ever …?
- Do you usually …?

> How often do you buy clothes online?

Vocabulary bank • page 108

Language focus 2 *(don't) want to, would(n't) like to, would prefer to*

1 Complete the examples from the listening on page 12.

Question	Answer
What do you [1].... **to** buy? What **would** you **like to** buy? [2].... you **prefer to** get a present?	I **want to / don't want to** buy some new shoes. I'**d** [3].... **to / wouldn't like to** buy a new games console. I'**d prefer to** get some money.

Grammar reference • page 100

2 1.10 Complete the conversations with *do(n't)* or *would(n't)*. Then listen and check.

1 A: [1].... you like to go shopping?
B: No, I [2].... prefer to stay at home.
2 A: What [3].... you want to do this afternoon?
B: I [4].... like to go to the new shopping mall.
3 A: I'm saving my money at the moment. I [5].... like to buy a new skateboard.
B: [6].... you prefer to buy it in a shop or online?
4 A: When you're older, [7].... you like to work in a shopping centre?
B: No, I [8].... .

Get it right!

Remember we use the infinitive after ***would like***, NOT *-ing*.
I would like ***to go*** *to the cinema.* ✓
~~*I would like going ...*~~ ✗

(not) enough + noun

3 Look at these examples from the listening on page 12. Write *enough* in the correct place.

1 I'd like to buy a new games console but I haven't got money.
2 I've nearly got money.

Grammar reference • page 100

Say it right! • page 96

4 Rewrite the sentences with *enough*.

1 My cousin wants to buy some new sunglasses but she hasn't got money.
My cousin wants to buy some new sunglasses but she hasn't got enough money.
2 I'd like to watch a film but I haven't got time.
3 We'd like to make hot chocolate but there isn't milk.
4 My dad thinks I don't do homework.
5 My brother is unhealthy because he doesn't do sport.
6 We want to start a football team but we haven't got players.

5 1.11 Complete the conversations with the words in the box. Then listen and check.

enough like prefer want

1 A: Would you [1].... to **go to the new shopping centre**?
B: I'm sorry I can't. I haven't got [2].... money.
2 A: Do you [3].... to **play football after school**?
B: I'd [4].... to **ride my bike. I don't like ball sports.**

Your turn

6 Work with a partner. Rewrite the conversations in Exercise 5 by changing the words in bold. Use these words or your own ideas.

go to my house the cinema the ice rink
a restaurant the underwater zoo watch a film
play tennis have a pizza play computer games

Would you like to go to my house after school?

I'm sorry I can't. I haven't got enough time.

Discover Culture

1 **You are going to watch a video about a tiger charity. How do you think it helps tigers? Why is it important to help them?**

Thailand

Find out about a tiger sanctuary in Thailand.

Discovery EDUCATION

1.2 Tiger sanctuary

2 **1.2 Watch the video and answer the questions.**

1. What is special about the people who work at the sanctuary?
2. How do they get money to buy food for the tigers?
3. How many tigers do they have at the moment?

3 **Test your memory. Which animals do you see in the video?**

monkey bear elephant owl dog duck
snake bat horse deer buffalo

4 **1.2 Watch the video again. Check your answers to Exercise 3 and choose the correct words.**

1. Tigers go to the sanctuary when they are **ill / old** or in danger.
2. Unfortunately, some people like **hunting / hurting** tigers.
3. These tigers **can / can't** live in the wild.
4. The tigers **are / are not** like pets.
5. Everyday they **run / eat** a lot!

Your turn

5 **Write answers to the questions.**

1. Are there any animal sanctuaries in your country?
2. What animals do they help?
3. Do people give money to help animals?
4. What wild animals have you got in your country?

6 **Work in small groups. Ask and answer the questions in Exercise 5.**

What wild animals have you got in your country?

Reading An article

1 **Look at the title of the article and the photos. What happens on *Red Nose Day*?**

2 1.12 **Read the article and check your ideas to Exercise 1.**

3 **Read the article again. Mark the sentences true (*T*) or false (*F*).**

1. Red Nose Day is every year. *False.*
2. Everybody gives the same money.
3. Some people wear red noses on this day.
4. Pupils sometimes wear unusual clothes to school.
5. In the UK, Red Nose Day helps people who need somewhere to live.
6. Red Nose Day is a very new charity day.

Explore adjective prefixes

4 **Find the opposite of *usual* in the text. How do we make it?**

5 **Add *un-* to the adjectives in the box. Then complete the sentences.**

~~usual~~ friendly fair tidy helpful happy

1. I like your dress. It's very different and *unusual* .
2. You look sad. Are you .... ?
3. There are things on the floor. My brother's room is .... .
4. Don't ask that man to show you. He's so .... .
5. They never smile or say hello. They're very .... .
6. My brother gets more pocket money than me. It's .... .

Vocabulary bank • page 108

Your turn

6 **Write your answers to the questions. Then ask and answer them with a partner.**

1. Would you like to work for a charity? Would you prefer to help animals or people?
2. Do you do charity events in your school? What?
3. What would you like to do on Red Nose Day?

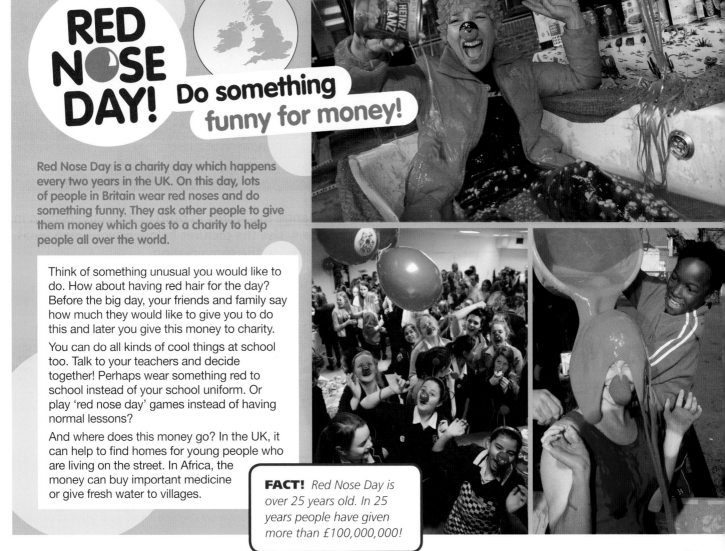

RED NOSE DAY! Do something funny for money!

Red Nose Day is a charity day which happens every two years in the UK. On this day, lots of people in Britain wear red noses and do something funny. They ask other people to give them money which goes to a charity to help people all over the world.

Think of something unusual you would like to do. How about having red hair for the day? Before the big day, your friends and family say how much they would like to give you to do this and later you give this money to charity.

You can do all kinds of cool things at school too. Talk to your teachers and decide together! Perhaps wear something red to school instead of your school uniform. Or play 'red nose day' games instead of having normal lessons?

And where does this money go? In the UK, it can help to find homes for young people who are living on the street. In Africa, the money can buy important medicine or give fresh water to villages.

FACT! *Red Nose Day is over 25 years old. In 25 years people have given more than £100,000,000!*

Speaking Shopping

Real talk: How do you spend your money?

1 1.3 **Watch the teenagers in the video. How do they spend their money? Use these words.**

phone ~~food~~ music going out with friends clothes comic books concert tickets video games

a) Speaker 1 *food*
b) Speaker 2 ....
c) Speaker 3 ....
d) Speaker 4 ....
e) Speaker 5 .... and ....
f) Speaker 6 .... and ....

2 **How do *you* spend your money? Ask and answer with your partner.**

3 1.13 **Listen to Matt talking to a shop assistant. What colour trainers would he like?**

4 1.13 **Complete the conversation with the useful language. Then listen and check your answers.**

Useful language

Can I try them on?
How much are they?
I'd like to buy ...
What size are you?
I'd prefer ...
I'll take them!

Matt:	Excuse me, [1].... some **trainers**.
Shop assistant:	What about these?
Matt:	[2].... a different colour. Have you got anything in **blue**?
Shop assistant:	Yes, do you like these?
Matt:	Yes! [3]....
Shop assistant:	They're **£59.99**.
Matt:	[4]....
Shop assistant:	Of course. [5]....
Matt:	I'm a size **40**, I think.
Shop assistant:	Here you are.
Shop assistant:	How are they?
Matt:	They're great. [6]....

5 **Practise the conversation in Exercise 4 with a partner.**

6 **Change the words in bold in the conversation in Exercise 4. Use the pictures below or your own ideas. Then, practise the conversation.**

Excuse me, I'd like to buy some jeans.

What about these?

Writing An email

1 **Look at the photo and read the emails. What help does Joey give Annie?**

Hi Annie,

I know the problem! First, decide how much money you want to spend and then think about what you'd like to do with your tablet. Would you like to watch videos or would you prefer to read books or magazines?

Remember some tablets are better for playing games and others are good for looking on the Internet.

Don't buy the first tablet you find! Have your friends or family got one? Ask them! Then try it so you can see which one you'd like. And don't forget to look online – the prices are often better!

I hope this helps.

See you soon,

Joey

From: Annie **Date:** Thursday 16 October 14:17

Hi Joey,

I'm saving for a tablet but I'm not sure what to buy. Can you help me?

Thanks,

Annie

2 **Order the things Joey does in his email.**

a make a suggestion
b begin the email *1*
c give some information
d end the email
e respond to the previous email

3 **Find the words Joey uses to do the things in Exercise 2.**

1 *begin the email – Hi Annie,*

Useful language

Imperatives

In an email, we often make suggestions. Use the imperative for a quick, informal way to do this:

- *Decide* how much money you want to spend.
- *Don't* buy the first tablet you find.

4 **Find five more examples of imperatives in Joey's email.**

5 **Complete the sentences with the imperatives from the box.**

Don't buy	Go	Read	Save	Try

1 .... your friends' tablets to see which one you'd like.
2 .... to an electronics shop and ask for advice.
3 .... reviews of new tablets.
4 .... enough money to buy a good tablet.
5 .... anything online if it is really cheap – it's probably not very good.

PLAN

6 **Read the email from Danny and make notes about what you want to say. Use the ideas in Exercise 2.**

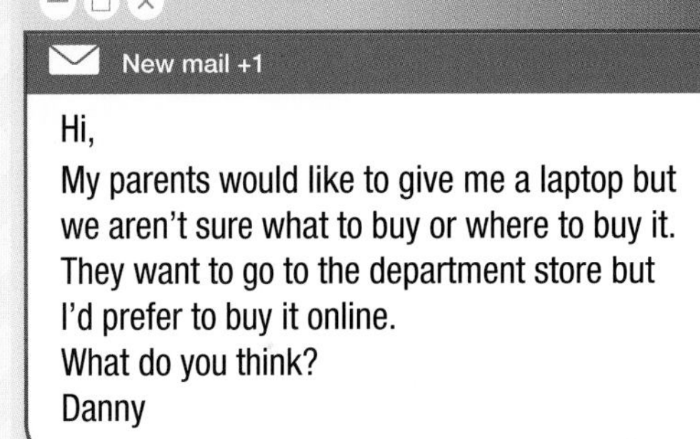

New mail +1

Hi,

My parents would like to give me a laptop but we aren't sure what to buy or where to buy it. They want to go to the department store but I'd prefer to buy it online.

What do you think?

Danny

WRITE

7 **Write your email. Use your notes and the language below.**

Hi
I know the problem.
First, … and then …
Would you like to … or would you prefer to …?
I hope this helps.
See you soon,

CHECK

8 **Can you say YES to these questions?**

- Have you got imperatives to make suggestions?
- Have you got the information from Exercise 2?
- Have you got the language from Exercise 7?

Our heroes

Discovery EDUCATION

In this unit ...

Vocabulary

- Jobs
- Adjectives of character
- Expressions with *make*
- The suffix *-ness*

Language focus

- *was/were*
- past simple: affirmative and negative
- past simple time expressions
- *was/were* and past simple questions

Unit aims

I can ...

- talk about different jobs.
- describe events in the past.
- understand information about present and past heroes.
- ask and answer questions about things in the past.
- give an opinion about something I'm not sure about.
- write a description of a person.

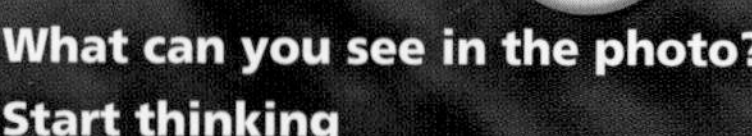

BE CURIOUS

What can you see in the photo?

Start thinking

- **What do you think happened before this photo?**
- **Who is the hero in the photo and why?**
- **Who are your heroes?**

Vocabulary Jobs

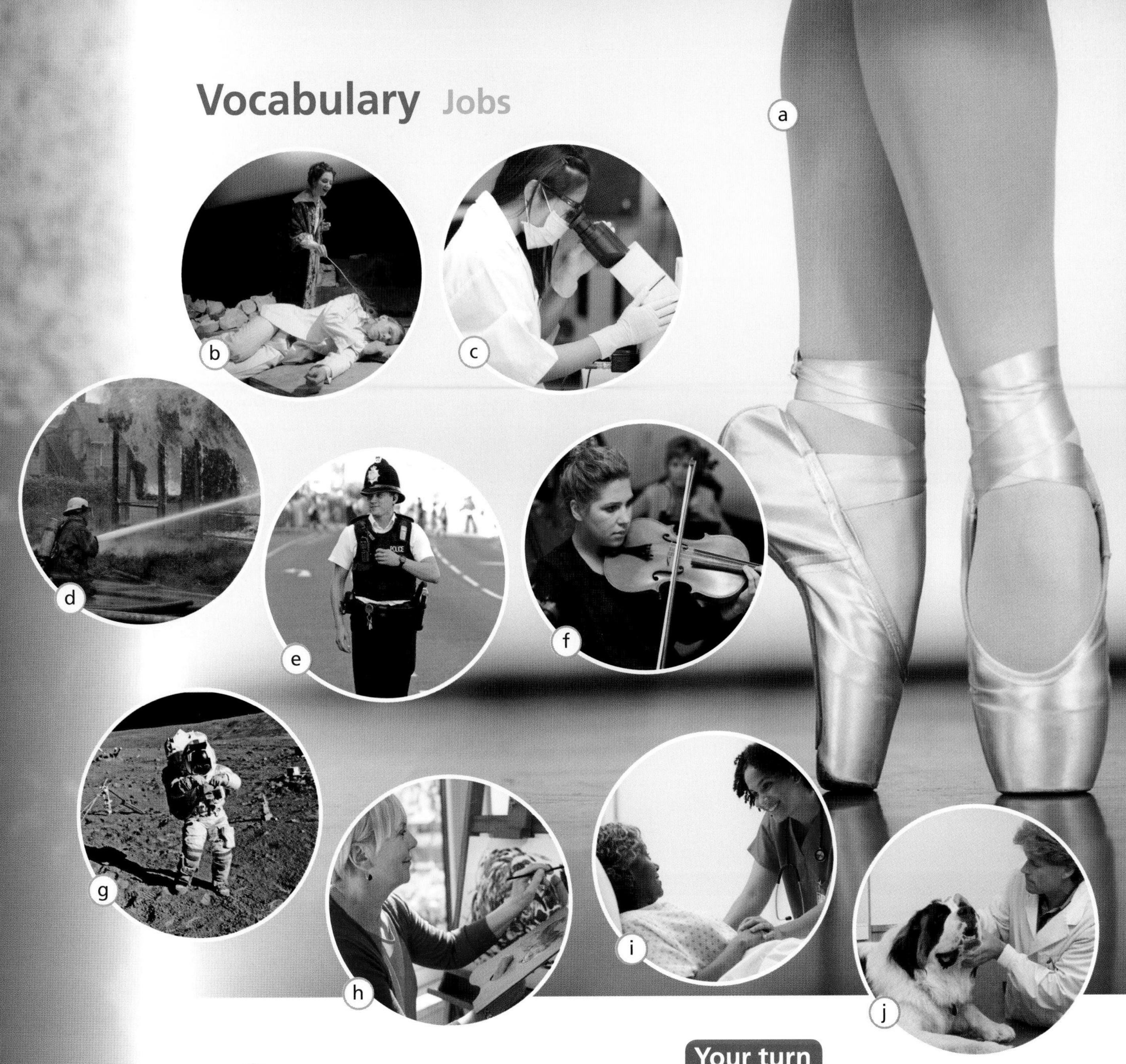

1 1.14 **Match the pictures with the words in the box. Then listen, check and repeat.**

dancer police officer musician actor nurse artist vet astronaut scientist firefighter

2 **Complete the table with the words in Exercise 1.**

Science	Artistic / Creative	Life savers
scientist		

Your turn

3 **Look at the jobs in Exercise 1 and write answers to the questions.**

1 Which two jobs would you like to do? Why?
2 Which two jobs would you not like to do? Why?

I'd like to be an artist because I love drawing and painting.

4 **Work with a partner. Ask and answer the questions in Exercise 3.**

Which job would you like to do?

I'd like to be an artist because I love drawing and painting. What about you?

Vocabulary bank • page 109

QUIZ OF THE MONTH

PEOPLE WHO MADE A DIFFERENCE

1 Christopher Columbus was born in Genoa over 500 years ago. He wanted to sail to Asia from Europe. He started his journey in 1492, but he didn't arrive in Asia because he made a mistake. Two months later he arrived in .... .

A The Caribbean Islands
B Brazil
C Canada

2 Anne Frank was a young Jewish girl living in Amsterdam over 80 years ago. During the Second World War, her family hid in a few small rooms in a house because the German army wanted to put Jewish people in prison. They were there for two years. Every day, Anne wrote about her life. In 1944, the Germans found Anne and her family and took them to Germany where she died in March 1945. What is the name of the book that she wrote?

A My Life at War
B A Girl's Life
C The Diary of a Young Girl

3 Tim Berners-Lee was an engineer but became interested in computers in the 1970s. He wrote a program that could connect computers across the world. He called it the World Wide Web and made history when he gave it to the world for free. He said, 'This is for everyone.' But when did the web go worldwide?

A in 1980
B in 1991
C in 2002

FACT! *Teachers can be heroes too. In 2012, Elaine Johnson, a primary school teacher from California, USA saved the lives of two students when she pulled them from a car that was on fire. Amazingly, the students weren't hurt.*

Reading A magazine quiz

1 Look at the people in the pictures. Who are they? Why are they famous?

2 1.15 Read the quiz and check your answers to Exercise 1.

3 Read the quiz again and answer the questions.

Explore expressions with *make*

4 Find three expressions with *make* in the text.

5 Complete the sentences with *make* and one of the words in the box.

a cake	~~mistakes~~	friends	a suggestion	history	sure

1 Do the exam carefully. Try not to *make mistakes* .
2 When I go on holiday, I often .... with the new people I meet.
3 People who change something in our world .... .
4 It's John's birthday tomorrow. Let's .... .
5 Before you close the door, ... you've got your keys.
6 Can I .... ? Let's go to the cinema on Saturday afternoon.

Vocabulary bank • page 109

Your turn

6 Think of a famous hero. Write your answers to the questions.

1 What's his/her name?
2 Where is he/she from?
3 Where does he/she live?
4 What does he/she do?
5 Why is he/she a hero?

7 Work with a partner. Ask and answer the questions about your hero in Exercise 6.

What's your hero's name?

Language focus 1 *was/were*

1 Complete the examples from the text on page 20.

	I / he / she / it	you / we / they
+	Anne Frank [1]…. a young Jewish girl.	They [2]…. there for two years.
–	America **wasn't** on Columbus' map.	Amazingly, the students [3]…. hurt.

Grammar reference • page 101

2 Choose the correct answer.

1 He **was / were / weren't** a famous tennis player 10 years ago.
2 You **were / wasn't / was** very good at sport at primary school.
3 I **were / weren't / was** at home at 8 o'clock last night.
4 My friends **were / was / wasn't** at football practice yesterday.
5 I **were / weren't / wasn't** at school last week. I **was / were / weren't** ill.
6 She **was / were / weren't** born in Ireland in 1991.

Past simple and time expressions

3 Complete the examples from the text on page 20.

+	He [1]…. his journey in 1492.
–	He [2]…. arrive in Asia.

Grammar reference • page 101

Say it right! • page 96

4 Complete the sentences in the past simple with the words in brackets.

1 I usually do my homework before dinner but yesterday, *I did my homework* (after dinner).
2 We normally have our lunch at school but on Monday …. (at home).
3 I often swim in the swimming pool but last summer, …. (in the lake).
4 I visit my grandparents on Sundays but last weekend …. (on Saturday).
5 My mum teaches at my brother's school but when I was little …. (at my school).
6 I study in the library every day now but three years ago I …. (once a week).

5 Complete the text with the verbs in brackets.

Marie Curie [1]…. (be) a scientist. She [2]…. (live) in Paris, France but she [3]…. (not be) French, she [4]…. (be) from Poland. She [5]…. (meet) her husband, Pierre, at university in Paris, and together they [6]…. (discover) radium. Many of the teachers at the university [7]…. (not want) Marie to teach there because she was a woman, but in 1906 she [8]…. (make) history and [9]…. (become) the first woman to teach at the university, three years after becoming the first woman to win a Nobel prize.

6 Order the time expressions in the box. Start with the most recent.

yesterday this morning when I was little
four days ago last weekend

Your turn

7 Think of some people you know. Write sentences about what they did and when. Use the events below and the time expressions in Exercise 6. Then compare your sentences with your partner.

went to school gave me a present
played a sport helped me went to a party
read a book went to a foreign country was ill

My best friend went to school this morning.

Learn about Yanna, a vet in South Africa.
- Why is Yanna's job special?
- Why did she become a vet?
- Why did she shoot the rhino in the video?

Listening A conversation

1 **Look at the advertisement. What is Young Heroes?**

2 1.18 **Listen to Laura talking to Harry and check your answer to Exercise 1.**

3 1.18 **Listen again and answer the questions.**

1 Who do they give prizes to?
2 How did the programme choose the winners?
3 What did Mike do last year?
4 What does Lisa do for other young people?
5 Is Alan still ill?
6 What does Alan do when he isn't studying?

Young Heroes
CHANNEL 5
7 PM – 9 PM
Tonight we give a special prize to three young heroes. Live music from One Direction and Beyoncé.

Vocabulary Adjectives of character

4 1.19 **Look at the pictures and complete the sentences with the words in the box. Then listen and check.**

brave	calm	cheerful	friendly	funny	kind	quiet	serious

1 Steven is very .... . He didn't say anything in class today.

2 Becky's really .... . She made us laugh a lot at the party.

3 Ben's very .... . We went to see a funny film and he didn't laugh at all.

4 Anna's really .... . She went on everything at the theme park!

5 Alice is so .... . When we went on holiday together, she was happy every day and smiled at everyone.

6 Jack was .... when the accident happened. He wasn't afraid and he called the police.

7 Andy is really .... . He made lots of new friends at summer camp.

8 Tania is very .... to animals. She gave a cat some food last week, and then she found it a home.

Your turn

5 **Use the adjectives in Exercise 4 to write sentences about five people you know.**

My little sister is brave. Last week, she caught three mice and six spiders.

6 **Work with a partner. Read your sentences from Exercise 5 but don't say the adjective. Can your partner guess the adjective?**

A: Last week, my sister caught three mice and six spiders.
B: She's brave!

Vocabulary bank • page 109

Language focus 2 *was/were*: questions

1 Complete the examples from the listing on page 22.

	I / he / she / it	you / we / they
Wh-	Who [1].... the third hero?	Who [2].... the winners?
Y/N ?	**Was** the show good?	**Were** you at school?
Short answers	Yes, it **was**. No, it **wasn't**.	Yes, we **were**. No, we **weren't**.

Grammar reference • page 101

2 Order the words to make questions with *was* and *were*.

1. at this time yesterday / Where / you / were?
2. time / you / at / were / this / school / What / morning?
3. were / at / Who / friends / primary / your / school?
4. born / you / When / were?
5. teacher / was / first / Who / your / English?
6. your / was / five / ago / favourite / What / TV programme / years?

3 Work with a partner. Ask and answer the questions in Exercise 2.

Past simple: questions

4 Complete the examples from the listening on page 22.

	I / he / she / it	you / we / they
Wh- ?	What **did** she [1].... ?	How **did** they [2].... them?
Y/N ?	**Did** he **win**?	[3].... you **watch** TV last night?
Short answers	Yes, he **did**. No, he **didn't**.	Yes, you **did**. No, you **didn't**.

Grammar reference • page 101

Get it right!

Use the infinitive without *to* with *did* in past simple questions and negatives:

*What **did** you **eat** yesterday?* ✓

~~*What did you ate yesterday?*~~ ✗

*I **didn't see** my cousin at the party.* ✓

~~*I didn't saw my cousin at the party.*~~ ✗

5 Read the answers. Then complete the questions.

1. What *did* you *have* for breakfast?
   I had toast and hot chocolate.
2. Where .... you .... your shoes?
   I bought them in the department store.
3. What time .... your mother .... home?
   She came home at 8 o'clock.
4. Who .... you .... to school with?
   I walked with my friends.
5. Where .... your parents .... before?
   They lived in Paris.
6. What .... your teacher .... at university?
   She studied Maths.

6 Write questions in the past simple.

1. When / you / start secondary school?
   When did you start secondary school?
2. Who / you / meet at the weekend?
3. Where / you / go on holiday last summer?
4. What / your family / watch on TV last night?
5. How / you / get to school this morning?
6. What sports / you / play yesterday?

Your turn

7 Write your answers to the questions in Exercise 6.

1. *I started it three years ago.*

8 Work with a partner. Ask and answer the questions in Exercise 6. Remember to ask for more information.

When did you start secondary school?

I started three years ago.

Did you enjoy the first day?

Yes, I did because I made some new friends.

Discover Culture

1 **Look at the picture. What job do you think the men do? Can you guess why they are heroes?**

San Jose Mine
Santiago

Find out about a mine rescue in Chile.

2.2 The Chilean Mine Rescue

2 **2.2 Watch the video and check your answers to Exercise 1. Then choose the correct options in the text below.**

In [1]**2010 / 2012**, there was a terrible accident. A giant rock fell and closed the San José mine with [2]**33 / 43** miners inside. Luckily, the miners found a safe place [3]**70 / 700** metres underground. The rescue workers made lots of holes to try to find the miners. Finally, [4]**69 / 79** days after the accident, the first man came out alive. The rescue worked. These brave men were suddenly [5]**national / international** heroes.

3 **Test your memory. Complete the sentences.**

1 The San José Mine is in the Atacama ...
2 The rock fell in front of the mine's ...
3 The camp was called *Esperanza* which means ...
4 The families knew the miners were OK because they wrote a ...
5 Families could see the miners because they had a ...
6 A million people all over the world watched the final ...

4 **2.2 Test your memory. Put the images in the order you see them in the video. Then watch again and check your answers.**

1 Rescue workers talk to the miners on the phone
2 The desert from the sky
3 A miner in hospital
4 The families' camp with posters and flags
5 The families hold flags and celebrate
6 A message on the drill

Your turn

5 **Work with a partner. Imagine you are journalists and you are going to interview the Chilean miners. Write questions in the past with the question words and verbs below or your own ideas.**

What Who When How Where

eat drink play sleep read
talk write walk feel

What did you eat? Did you play games?

6 **Work in small groups. Journalists ask your questions from Exercise 5 and miners answer. Then swap.**

What did you eat?

We had a little cold food with us. Then the rescue workers gave us some more food.

Reading A blog

1 **Look at the map and the photos. Where is Jamaica? Who are the people in the photos?**

2 1.20 **Read Danielle's blog and check your answers to Exercise 1.**

3 **Read the article again and answer the questions.**

1 How many people live in Jamaica?
2 What sorts of heroes does Danielle write about?
3 When do Jamaican children start doing sport at school?
4 What or who is *Champs*?
5 What type of music started in Jamaica?
6 What do Jamaican musicians often sing about?

Explore the suffix *-ness*

4 **Look at the article again. Find the noun from the adjectives *happy* and *sad*. Then answer the questions.**

1 What do we add to the adjective to make the noun?
2 What happens to the 'y' in *happy* when we make the noun?

5 **Complete the sentences with the noun of the adjective in brackets.**

1 Many musicians write songs about love and *sadness*. (sad)
2 Please put your books on the shelf. .... is very important. (tidy)
3 I think .... is more important than money. (happy)
4 Singing is my .... . I'm not very good at it. (weak)
5 The band didn't play because of .... . (ill)
6 I'll never forget my grandma's .... when she listened to my problems. (kind)

Vocabulary bank • page 109

Your turn

6 **Write your answers to the questions. Then ask and answer them with a partner.**

1 Who's your favourite sportsperson? Where's he/she from? What sports does he/she do?
2 Who's your favourite musician? Where's he/she from? What kind of music does he/she play?

DANIELLE SMITH'S BLOG OF ALL THINGS JAMAICAN

A SMALL ISLAND FULL OF BIG HEROES

14 OCTOBER

I live on the small Caribbean island of Jamaica. Like many of the 3 million people here, sport and music are very important to me. Perhaps that's why so many sports and music heroes come from our island.

We start playing sports seriously at a very young age. Even at primary school we follow an athletics programme. At secondary school, there's the school athletics championship, or 'Champs'. Every year, about 25,000 people watch some of the heroes of tomorrow. Usain Bolt, the Olympic Gold Medallist, is from Jamaica and he once entered this championship.

As for music, in the 1960s, my own hero Bob Marley introduced reggae to the world. He didn't only sing about happiness, love and sadness. He also sang about how people live and their problems. Today, even our youngest musicians write about our life here on the island. When you next listen to a song from Jamaica, don't forget it's probably about us, our life and our culture!

FACT! *The Jamaican bobsleigh team became heroes when they entered the Winter Olympics in 1988. Strange! Jamaica is famous for its sun but not for its snow!*

Speaking Speculating

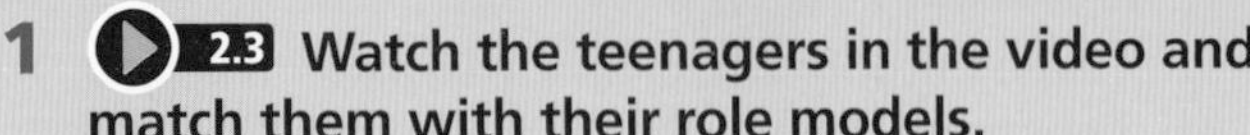

Real talk: Who's your role model and why?

1 2.3 Watch the teenagers in the video and match them with their role models.

a) Speaker 1
b) Speaker 2
c) Speaker 3
d) Speaker 4
e) Speaker 5
f) Speaker 6

1 a friend because he saved his sister from a fire.
2 a famous actor because she's good at her job and helps children.
3 a teacher because her lessons are really interesting.
4 an athlete because he can run fast.
5 someone in his family because he's kind and hardworking.
6 someone in her family because she dances well.

2 **Who's *your* role model and why? Ask and answer with your partner.**

3 1.21 **Listen to Darren and Louise talking about the woman in the photo above. What job do they think she does?**

4 1.21 **Complete the conversation with the useful language. Then listen again and check your answers.**

Useful language

She looks (very kind).
… that's possible.
She may be (a vet).
She definitely (works with animals).
I reckon she's (a vet).

Darren: What do you think she does?
Louise: I'm not sure.
Darren: 1.... very kind.
Louise: Yes, and friendly.
Darren: 2.... an artist.
Louise: Yes, 3.... . Or she may be a vet because there's a gorilla in the photo.
Darren: Yes, that's true. 4.... works with animals.
Louise: Yes, 5.... a vet or a scientist.
Darren: Me too.
Louise: Let's ask the teacher.

5 **Work with a partner. Practise the conversation in Exercise 4.**

6 **Work with a partner. Prepare a conversation like the one in Exercise 4. Use the photos below and the useful language. Practise the conversation with your partner.**

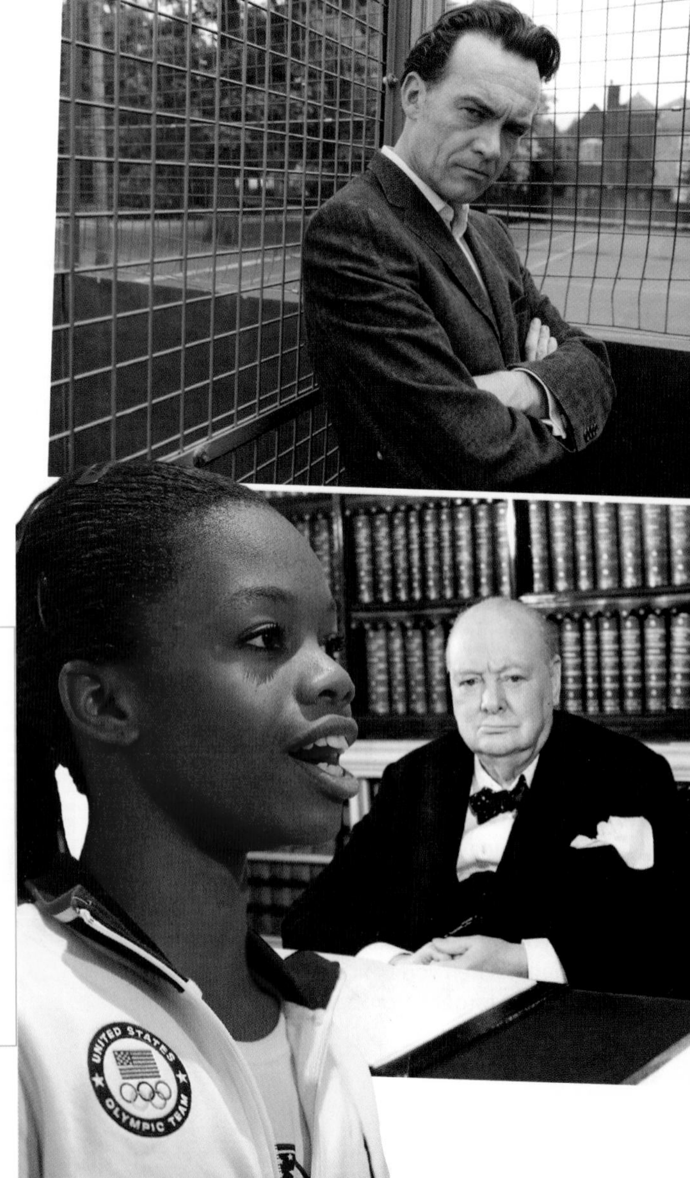

Writing A description of a person you admire

1 **Look at the photo and read Jennifer's description. Is Jennifer's hero famous?**

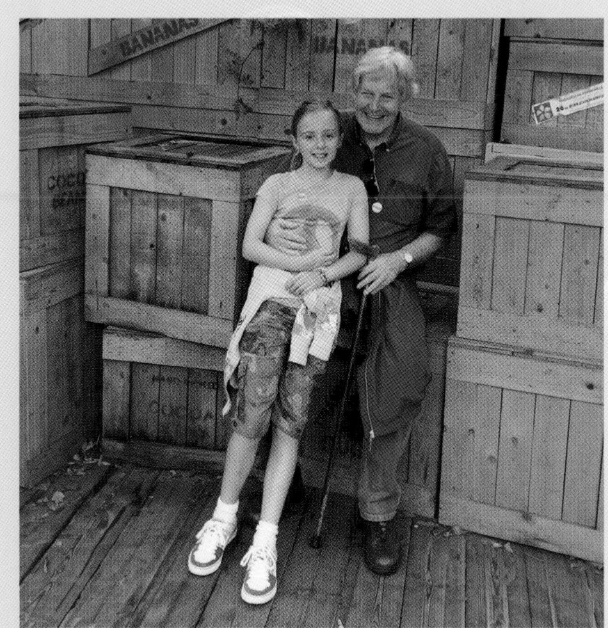

Although most people have got heroes like Nelson Mandela or Usain Bolt, my hero is my granddad. He was born 80 years ago so he's very old. When he was a young boy, his parents died so he lived with his aunt, uncle and cousins in Manchester. Life wasn't easy for them because they never had enough money.

When he was 13, my granddad left school and started working. He wanted to be a vet so he studied at night after work as well. He worked really hard and he became a vet when he was 25. It was his dream job.

I like him because he's funny, friendly and kind to everyone, and I admire him because he worked hard to achieve his dream.

I would like to be like him when I'm older.

By Jennifer Thompson

2 **Read Jennifer's description and answer the questions.**

1 Who is Jennifer's hero?
2 Where did he live?
3 What was his job?
4 Why is he a hero?
5 What's her hero like?

Useful language

Connectors

We often use connectors when we write descriptions:

- ***Although*** *most people have got heroes like Nelson Mandela or Usain Bolt, my hero is my granddad.*
- *I like him* **because** *he's funny, friendly and kind to everyone.*
- *He was born 80 years ago* **so** *he's very old.*
- *He wanted to be a vet so he studied at night after work* ***as well****.*

3 **Complete the sentences with *as well, although, because* or *so.***

1 My hero is my teacher .... I learn a lot in her class.
2 They help with the local football team and organise the youth club .... .
3 My best friend helped me when I was having problems .... I'm going to buy her a present.
4 My aunt gives a lot of money to charities .... she never talks about it.
5 I would like to be a vet .... I like helping animals.
6 David wants to go to university .... he doesn't know which one to go to.

PLAN

4 **Make notes about a person you admire. Use the questions in Exercise 2.**

WRITE

5 **Write your description. Use your notes from Exercise 4, and the language below.**

My hero is …
He/She was born …
When he/she was …
I like him/her because …
I admire him/her because …
I would like to be like him/her when I'm older.

CHECK

6 **Can you say YES to these questions?**

- Have you got connectors to add more information?
- Have you got the information from Exercise 4?
- Have you got the language from Exercise 5?

1–2 Review

Vocabulary

1 Match the pictures with the shops in the box.

sports shop   chemist   electronics shop   clothes shop   newsagent   music shop

a 
b 

c 
d 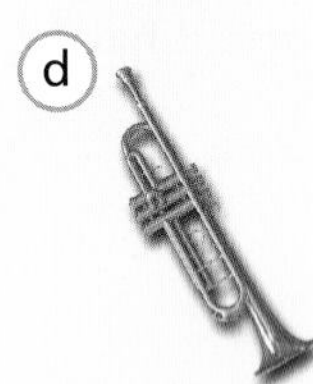
e 
f 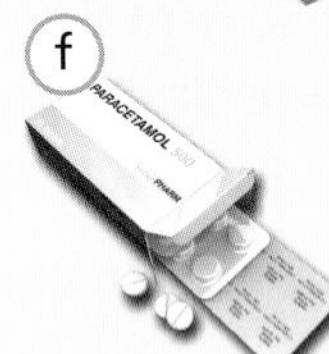

2 Complete the sentences with the words in the box.

borrow   buy   earn   save   sell   spend

1 I'm going to the bookshop to .... a book.
2 My brother wants to .... his old laptop for €50.
3 Can I .... some money? I can give it back to you tomorrow!
4 How much money do you .... on sweets every week?
5 I sometimes help my dad in the garden to .... extra pocket money.
6 I'm not eating sweets because I'm trying to .... money for a new bike.

3 Look at the pictures and write the jobs.

1  ....
2  ....
3  ....
4  ....
5  ....
6  ....

4 Match the sentences with the adjectives.

calm   cheerful   funny   brave   quiet   serious

1 I'm not scared of spiders, big dogs or dentists. I'm .... .
2 My classmate Max never laughs. He's very .... .
3 I'm a nervous person and I worry about things. I'm not very .... .
4 My uncle is really good at telling jokes. He's very .... .
5 My sister talks a lot. It's difficult for her to be .... .
6 My little sister always smiles and laughs. She's very .... .

Explore vocabulary

5 Choose the correct answers.

1 I'm wearing two sweaters, a coat and gloves because it's **freezing / awful**.
2 That new shopping centre has got more than 1,000 shops. It's **huge / boiling**.
3 I didn't like that new restaurant. The food was **brilliant / awful**.
4 We can't play football because it's 36°C outside. It's **brilliant / boiling**.
5 I loved the concert. I thought the singer was **brilliant / freezing**.

6 Complete the sentences. Add the prefix *un-* or the suffix *-ness* to the words in brackets.

1 I never go to that shop because the shop assistants are very .... . (helpful)
2 Why has Jack got a bigger piece of cake? That's .... . (fair)
3 I think .... is very important in a friend. (kind)
4 I would like to earn a lot of money but .... is more important. (happy)
5 It's May and it's snowing! That's .... . (usual)
6 My teacher says that .... is very important. I don't agree. (tidy)

7 Complete the sentences with the correct form of *make* and one of these words.

sure   a cake   friends   history   a suggestion   mistakes

1 When you leave the house, ... you've got your keys.
2 I'd like to .... . Why don't you try on those shoes before you buy them?
3 My friends always do their homework quickly so they .... .
4 We haven't got enough eggs. We can't .... .
5 I'm a friendly person so I .... very easily.
6 I'd love to do something important for the world and .... .

Language focus

1 Complete the text with the present continuous form of the verbs in brackets.

Lisa and Clare [1]…. (not study) today. They [2]…. (shop). They [3]…. (look) for new dresses for a party on Saturday. Lisa [4]…. (try) on a red dress. Clare [5]…. (not try) on dresses at the moment. She [6]…. (take) a photo of a dress to send to her mum.

2 Complete the sentences with the present simple or present continuous form of the verbs in brackets.

1 We …. History at the moment. (study)
2 What time …. he usually …. to school? (go)
3 My parents often …. TV in the evening. (watch)
4 Peter and Susana …. for clothes right now. (shop)
5 …. you …. dinner now? (eat)
6 They …. to the cinema every weekend. (not go)

3 Choose the correct answers.

1 **A:** Would you [1]**want / like** to have a pizza before we go home?
B: I'm sorry I can't. I haven't got [2]**enough time / time enough**.
2 **A:** I [3]**wouldn't / don't** want to go to the ice rink.
B: I agree. I'd [4]**prefer / want** to go to the cinema.
3 **A:** I haven't got [5]**enough money / money enough** to go to the underwater zoo.
B: Don't worry. I don't [6]**like / want** to go there today.

4 Complete the text with the correct past simple form of the verbs in the box.

buy go move leave be (x4) want not be not live study

Joanna [1]…. born in Canada, but she [2]…. there for very long. When she [3]…. three, her parents [4]…. to England. They [5]…. a house in South London. Joanna [6]…. to school in Chelsea. Unfortunately, she [7]…. very good at subjects like Science and Maths, but she [8]…. good at Art. When she [9]…. school, she [10]…. Art and Design at university. Her parents [11]…. a little sad at first – they [12]…. her to be a doctor. But now they're happy because she's happy!

5 Complete the questions with *was*, *were* or *did*.

1 Where …. you born?
2 What languages …. Lisa study?
3 When …. you go to France?
4 …. you study Biology at school?
5 …. Mike good at Maths?
6 …. your parents at home last night?

6 Complete the sentences with the time expressions in the box.

last night an hour ago when I was little at the weekend yesterday

1 I had lunch at 1 pm, now it's 2 pm. I had lunch …. .
2 Jack started school on Monday. Today is Tuesday. He started school …. .
3 Helen was at home on Saturday and Sunday. She was at home …. .
4 I watched the film yesterday at 8 pm. I watched the film …. .
5 We moved here in 2006. I was 4 years old. We moved here …. .

Language builder

7 Choose the correct answers.

Nina: Hi, Debbie. [1] *b* anything at the moment?
Debbie: No, not really. Why?
Nina: They [2]…. a market at the sports centre today. [3]…. you like to come with me?
Debbie: Yes, please! I [4]…. markets. I [5]…. interesting things.
Nina: Me too! I went to a market two weeks [6]…. and I [7]…. a baseball cap and some sunglasses.
Debbie: [8]…. they expensive?
Nina: No, not at all. I [9]…. spend more than £10. I wanted to buy some trainers but I didn't have [10]…. .

	a	b
1	a Do you do	b Are you doing
2	a 're having	b have
3	a Would	b Do
4	a love	b loves
5	a often find	b 'm often finding
6	a past	b ago
7	a am buying	b bought
8	a Were	b Did
9	a didn't	b wasn't
10	a money enough	b enough money

Speaking

8 Complete the phrases with the words in the box.

looks possible think may reckon sure

1 What do you …. she does?
2 I'm not …. .
3 She …. be a nurse.
4 She …. very kind.
5 I …. she's a teacher.
6 That's …. .

3 Strange stories

In this unit ...

Mystery in the mountains **p33**

A story from under the sea **p36**

Strange events **p38**

CLIL Behind the scenes **p118**

Vocabulary

- Action verbs
- Adverbs of manner
- Expressions with *look*
- Nouns with *-er*

Language focus

- Past continuous
- Past continuous vs. past simple
- *could(n't)*

Unit aims

I can ...

- tell a story using action verbs.
- understand strange stories.
- talk about my activities in the past.
- describe how I do things.
- talk about the things I could and couldn't do when I was younger.
- tell someone my news.
- write a story.

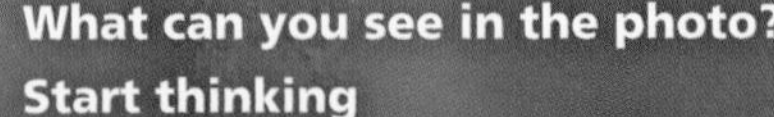

What can you see in the photo?

Start thinking

- **Do you think this is a real photo? Why/Why not?**
- **What other strange things do you know about?**
- **Can you think of an explanation for these mysteries?**

Vocabulary Action verbs

1 **Look at the story about a thief. What did the thief steal?**

2 1.22 **Match the pictures with the words in the box. Then listen, check and repeat.**

catch	chase	climb	hide	fall over
jump	run away	throw		

3 **Complete the sentences with the past simple form of the verbs in Exercise 2.**

1. The thief ..*ran*.. away from our car.
2. I .... the thief.
3. The thief .... into a garden.
4. The thief .... his bag over a wall.
5. The thief .... over a wall.
6. The thief .... the bag.
7. The thief .... .
8. I .... the thief.

Your turn

4 **Work with a partner. Cover the sentences in Exercise 3. Then ask and answer questions about the story.**

What happened in picture 1?

The thief ran away from the car.

5 **Cover the pictures and write down the 8 sentences about the story.**

➔ **Vocabulary bank** • page 110

Reading A newspaper article

1 Work with a partner. Look at the pictures. What do you think happened in the story?

2 1.23 Read the newspaper article and check your ideas to Exercise 1.

HOME WORLD UK BUSINESS EDUCATION

TREASURE IN THE PARK

Pupils from Parkland School in Leeds were surprised last week when they were cleaning the park. They were looking for rubbish when they found something that looked like treasure!

'I was looking after their bags when I heard someone shout by the lake. I ran over and one of the children was jumping and pointing at a large bag. They weren't laughing but they were really excited,' said their teacher, Mrs Gibson. 'I phoned the police immediately.'

The police looked in the bag. It was full of expensive objects like watches and clocks, and even some gold. There were also some old photos, a Hungarian passport, two train tickets to Berlin and an old newspaper from 1956.

But where did these things come from? Who did they belong to? What were they doing there?

Police detective Stuart Bolan said, 'This morning I spoke to police in Hungary and they are trying to find the owner of the passport. The bag was in the park for a very long time so it really is a mystery.'

Were the children still talking about it a week later? 'They are very excited and are going to do a project on what they found,' said Mrs Gibson.

3 Read the text again and answer the questions.

1 What school did the children go to?
2 Where did they find the treasure?
3 What did the teacher do when she saw the bag?
4 Who opened the bag?
5 What was inside the bag?
6 Who did the police speak to about the objects?

Explore expressions with *look*

4 Find four examples of *look* + preposition in the newspaper article. Then complete the sentences with the correct preposition.

1 I was looking ...*for*... my keys, when I found my mobile phone.
2 Can you look .... the kitchen for my bag?
3 My aunt is working so I'm looking .... my little cousin.
4 I'm not sure what it is but it looks .... an old boot.

Vocabulary bank • page 110

Your turn

5 Look at the text. Write your own answers to the three questions in bold in the fourth paragraph.

6 Work in small groups. Compare your answers to the questions in Exercise 5 and decide which is your favourite.

I think thieves stole these objects.

I agree. But where did they come from?

FACT! *Four months before the 1966 World Cup in England, a thief stole the World Cup trophy and hid it inside some newspaper at the bottom of a garden. A dog called Pickles found it seven days later while he was walking with his owner. Both Pickles and his owner received a reward!*

Language focus 1 Past continuous: affirmative and negative

1 **Complete the examples from the text on page 32.**

	I / he / she / it	you / we / they
+	I [1].... **looking** after their bags.	They **were** [2].... for rubbish.
–	I **wasn't watching** the children.	They [3].... **laughing**.

Grammar reference • page 102

2 **Complete the police report with the past continuous form of the verbs in brackets.**

POLICE REPORT

Case No: 76543
Date and Time: 21 May 11 am

Police officer: Alfred Baker
Name of witness: Jim Hanson

Information:
What were you doing at the time?
When my friends found the bag, I [1]*was climbing* (climb) a tree and Danny [2].... (hide) behind that wall because Max [3].... (chase) us. Our teacher [4].... (stand) over there. She wasn't happy with us because we [5].... (not help) the others. Our classmates [6].... (not play), they [7].... (look) for rubbish and they [8].... (throw) empty cans and bottles into a bag.

Past continuous: questions

3 **Complete the examples from the text on page 32.**

	I / he / she / it	you / we / they
Wh- ?	What **was** Danny **doing**?	What **were** they [1].... there?
Y/N ?	**Was** she **looking** after the bag?	[2].... the children still **talking** about it?
Short answers	Yes, she **was**. No, she **wasn't**.	Yes, they **were**. No, they **weren't**.

Grammar reference • page 102

4 1.24 **Complete the conversation with the past continuous form of the verbs in brackets. Then listen and check your answers.**

Detective: What [1]*were* you *doing* (do) between 8 and 8.30 last night?
Schoolboy: I [2].... (look) at my Maths book.
Detective: Why [3].... you .... (study) Maths?
Schoolboy: Because I've got an exam tomorrow.
Detective: Where [4].... you .... (sit)?
Schoolboy: In my bedroom.
Detective: [5].... you .... (talk) to anyone at the same time?
Schoolboy: No, I [6].... (do) it alone.

Say it right! • page 96

Your turn

5 **Write questions for your partner with the past continuous. Use these times or your own ideas.**

5 pm last Wednesday 2 pm on Saturday
yesterday 11 am last night 7 pm
8 am this morning

What were you doing at 2 pm on Saturday?
Were you having lunch?

6 **Work with a partner. Ask and answer your questions from Exercise 5.**

What were you doing at 2 pm on Saturday?

I was finishing my homework.

Learn about an archaeologist's discovery.
- What did the archaeologist and his team find?
- What did he discover about the woman?
- Why do you think she travelled so far?

Listening A strange story

1 **Look at Liz's status update and the pictures. Why did Liz say "Goodbye Granny" in the shop?**

Liz Matthews posted 45 minutes ago
Don't say "Goodbye Granny" to the old lady in the cake shop!!

2 1.25 **Listen to Liz telling her friend Mel what happened to her. Check your ideas to Exercise 1.**

3 1.25 **Listen again. Mark the sentences true (*T*) or false (*F*).**

1 Liz's brother's birthday is today.
2 When Liz got to the shop, it was empty.
3 An old lady started talking to Liz outside the cake shop.
4 Liz paid £17 for the cake.
5 Liz bought her cake and the cakes for the old lady too.

Vocabulary Adverbs of manner

4 **Look at the examples from the listening and answer the questions.**

- An old lady was standing **quietly** next to me …
- The others were talking **loudly**.

1 Are the words in bold adjectives or adverbs?
2 What do we usually add to adjectives to make adverbs?

Get it right!

Remember these adverbs are irregular:
good → well, fast → fast, hard → hard

5 1.26 **Complete the sentences with the correct form of the adjectives in brackets. Then listen, check and repeat.**

a He cooks very *badly* (bad).

b The insect moved .... (slow) across the leaf.

c I carried the expensive glasses very .... (careful).

d The children were playing very .... (happy).

e I got dressed .... (quick) and went out.

f She answered all of the questions .... (easy).

g He paints very .... (good).

h She opened the door .... (quiet).

Your turn

6 **Write your answers to the questions.**

1 Do you always do your homework carefully?
2 Can you speak English well?
3 Do you get dressed for school quickly?
4 Is there anything you do badly?
5 Do you always speak in class quietly?
6 What can you do easily?

7 **Work with a partner. Ask and answer the questions from Exercise 6.**

Vocabulary bank • page 110

Language focus 2 Past simple vs. continuous

1 Look at the examples from the listening on page 34. Then complete rules 1 and 2 with *past simple* or *past continuous*.

- Something strange **happened** to me today while I **was shopping**.
- When I got to the cake shop, four people **were waiting**.

We use:
the [1].... to talk about activities in progress at a moment in the past.
the [2].... to talk about a short, finished action which happens in the middle of another activity.

Grammar reference • page 102

Get it right!

Use *when*, not *while*, to talk about something that happens at a point in time.
~~*While the phone rang.*~~ ✗
When the phone rang. ✓

2 Write sentences in past simple and continuous with *when* or *while* and the words below.

1 I / watch / TV / best friend / call
2 My dad / drive / home from work / car / suddenly / stop
3 I / walk / home from school / start / rain
4 I / see / you / you / wait / at the bus stop
5 My mum / read / a book / my brother / come home

3 Write questions with the past continuous or past simple form of the verb in brackets.

1 *Was* it *raining* (rain) when you woke up this morning?
2 .... your phone .... (ring) while you were having breakfast?
3 .... anything strange .... (happen) while you were going to school?
4 When you got to school, ... your friends .... (play) football?
5 When you went into the classroom, ... your teacher .... (write) on the board?
6 While you were listening to the teacher, ... you .... (look) out of the window?

Your turn

4 Work with a partner. Ask and answer the questions in Exercise 3. Did you have the same kind of morning?

Was it raining when you woke up this morning?

No, it wasn't but I woke up very early. Was it raining when you woke up?

could(n't)

5 Complete the examples from the listening on page 34 with *could* or *couldn't* and the verb in brackets.

+	I [1].... (play) it well when I was younger.
−	I [2].... (not hear) her very well.

Grammar reference • page 102

6 Which of the things in the box could you do when you were at primary school? Write sentences with *could* or *couldn't* and an adverb from page 34.

ride a bike | swim 25 metres | play a musical instrument | use a computer | speak two languages | sing | play your favourite sport

I could swim 25 metres quickly but I couldn't speak English well.

Your turn

7 Work with a partner. Ask and answer questions about the things in Exercise 6.

Could you swim 25 metres when you were in primary school?

Yes, I could swim 25 metres quickly.

Discover Culture

1 Look at the pictures and answer the questions.

1 What is different about the two pictures?
2 How do you think life in the two places is different?

2 3.2 Watch the first part of the video (0.00–1.17) and check your answers to Exercise 1. What are the names of the two places?

Find out about a lost city under the water.

Discovery EDUCATION

3.2 A story from under the sea

3 3.2 Watch the second part and complete Kihachiro Aratake's story.

This is Kihachiro Aratake – he's a [1].... . He was diving near the [2].... of Yonaguni when he found something amazing. It looked like a small [3].... under the water. It had [4]...., steps and tall towers. One stone had strange marks – was it ancient writing? Some [5].... think this structure is over 10,000 years old. They say it was once above the water.

4 Test your memory. Mark the sentences true (*T*) or false (*F*). Correct the false sentences.

1 Yonaguni is very close to Japan.
2 An old man is telling stories to some children.
3 Some people are dancing.
4 Kihachiro is with some friends on the boat.
5 He swims down the 'streets' of the underwater city.
6 There are lots of fish swimming around the ancient stones.

5 3.2 Watch the video again. Check your answers to Exercise 4 and choose the best summary for the video.

1 Yonaguni is a secret place where people go on holiday.
2 Yonaguni is a calm place where people have a lot of time to do what they like.
3 Yonaguni is mysterious and we don't know much about its ancient stories.

Your turn

6 Work with a partner. Ask and answer the questions.

1 What are the good things about living in a big capital city?
2 What are the good things about living on a small island?
3 Are there any mysterious places in your country like the underwater city? Where are they? What is their story?

Reading An article

1 **Look at the map and the photo. Where is Easter Island? What can you see in the picture? Who do you think built the statues?**

2 1.27 **Read the article and match the questions with the paragraphs.**

a Was life on the island always easy?
b Where is Easter Island?
c Who built the stone statues?
d Why is it called Easter Island?

3 **Read the text again and order the events.**

a There wasn't enough food.
b Explorers called the island Easter Island.
c People arrived on the island from Polynesia.
d The islanders built large stone statues.
e 111 people lived on the island.
f People started fighting each other.

Explore nouns with *-er*

4 **Complete the table with *-er* nouns. The first three are in the article.**

	noun with *-er*		noun with *-er*
explore	1 *explorer*	paint	5 ....
farm	2	build	6 ....
island	3	shop	7 ....
swim	4	photograph	8 ....

Vocabulary bank • page 110

Your turn

5 **Work in small groups. Ask and answer the questions.**

1 Would you like to live on Easter Island? Why/Why not?
2 Why do you think people from Polynesia travelled to Easter Island?
3 How do you think the islanders moved the statues next to the sea?

The Mystery of EASTER ISLAND

1 ....
When explorers landed on Easter Sunday, 5 April 1722, they called this island, Easter Island. They found some unusual things there; they weren't alone – people were living on the island and there were about 900 large stone statues.

2 ....
Easter Island is about 4,000km from any other country. Now you can fly there in about five hours from Chile but when the first people arrived from Polynesia between the years AD 300 and 1000, the only way to get there was a very long journey by boat.

3 ....
For thousands of years, life was easy for the people on Easter Island. At first, they were successful farmers and they also caught fish. At one time, around 12,000 people lived here. But at the start of the 17th century, the people were fighting each other because there wasn't enough food. In 1877, instead of over 10,000 people, there were only 111 left.

4 ....
When things were better, the islanders built the statues. Then they moved the statues so that they were next to the sea. All the statues had eyes so they could watch over the people on Easter Island.

FACT! *The statues are very heavy. Some weigh over 80,000 kgs. The islanders moved some of the statues 16 km to the sea.*

Speaking Telling someone your news

Real talk: What's an interesting or unusual thing that happened to you recently?

1 3.3 **Watch the teenagers in the video and put the sentences in the correct order.**

a) I lost my cat.
b) I scored the winning goal.
c) There was some chocolate on everybody's desk.
d) My lunch wasn't there. *1*
e) We were wearing the same shirt.
f) The lock on my bike wasn't there.

2 **What's an interesting or unusual thing that happened to *you* recently? Ask and answer with your partner.**

3 1.28 **Listen to Alice telling Lisa an interesting story. What did Alice win?**

4 1.28 **Complete the conversation with the useful language. Then, listen and check your answers.**

Useful language

Really? What?	How/That's weird!
What did you say?	What happened next?
Something strange happened	What did you do?

Alice: [1]…. this morning!
Lisa: [2]….
Alice: Well, I was walking into class when my phone rang.
Lisa: [3]….
Alice: Well, I answered it and a woman I didn't know started speaking.
Lisa: [4]….
Alice: She asked 'Is that Alice Bradman?' I said, 'yes'. And then she said, 'Alice, you're the winner in our photography competition.'
Lisa: Wow! [5]….
Alice: I said 'Great! Thank you very much!'
Lisa: Cool! But Alice, you never take photos.
Alice: I know and I never enter competitions!
Lisa: Oh! [6]…. ! What did you win?
Alice: A new digital camera!

5 **Work with a partner. Practise the conversation in Exercise 4.**

6 **Think of an interesting story. Use the useful language to ask and answer questions about your story with your partner.**

7 **Change partners. Take turns to tell each other your interesting story.**

Something strange happened this morning

Really? What?

Well, I was…

What did you do?

Writing A story

1 Look at the picture and read the story. Who is the man in the picture and what is he doing?

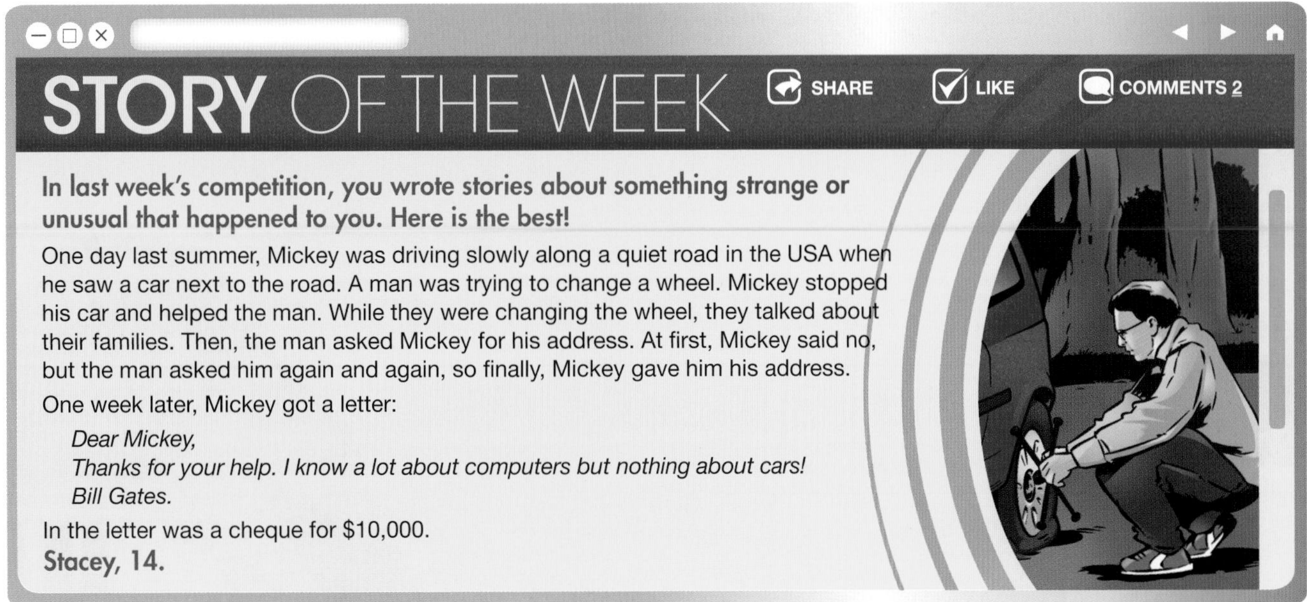

In last week's competition, you wrote stories about something strange or unusual that happened to you. Here is the best!

One day last summer, Mickey was driving slowly along a quiet road in the USA when he saw a car next to the road. A man was trying to change a wheel. Mickey stopped his car and helped the man. While they were changing the wheel, they talked about their families. Then, the man asked Mickey for his address. At first, Mickey said no, but the man asked him again and again, so finally, Mickey gave him his address.

One week later, Mickey got a letter:

Dear Mickey,
Thanks for your help. I know a lot about computers but nothing about cars!
Bill Gates.

In the letter was a cheque for $10,000.

Stacey, 14.

2 Answer the questions about the story.

1 When did the story happen?
2 Where did the story happen?
3 Who were the people in the story?
4 What happened in the beginning, in the middle and at the end of the story?

Useful language

Sequencing language 1

We use sequencing language to …

- start a story (***One day** last summer, …*)
- order events (***At first,** Mickey said no.*)
- finish a story (***Finally,** Mickey gave him his address.*)

3 Find more examples of sequencing language in the text in Exercise 1.

4 Complete the paragraph with the words in the box.

Finally	first	~~one~~	then	when	While

[1] *One* afternoon I was doing my homework quietly in my bedroom [2] …. I heard a strange noise outside. At [3] …., I didn't want to go outside, but [4] …. I opened the door and went into the garden. There was a very small dog. [5] …. I was playing with the dog, my mum came home. She was laughing. Five minutes later, my dad and sister arrived. They were laughing too. [6] …., I understood. The dog was my birthday present!

PLAN

5 Make notes about something strange or unusual that happened to you. It can be true or invented. Use the questions in Exercise 2.

WRITE

6 Write your story. Use your notes from Exercise 5, and the language below.

One day/night last week/month/year…
He/she was …ing when …
Then, …
While he/she was …ing …
At first, … but …
So finally, …
Two days/weeks/months later …

CHECK

7 Can you say YES to these questions?

- Have you got sequencing language to show the order the events happened?
- Have you got the information from Exercise 5?
- Have you got the language from Exercise 6?

4 At home

Discovery EDUCATION

In this unit ...

BE CURIOUS

What can you see in the photo?

Start thinking

- **Who do you think lives here?**
- **Why do you think they live there?**
- **Would you like to live here? Why/Why not?**

Vocabulary

- Things in the home
- Household appliances
- Expressions with *do*
- Verbs with *up* or *down*

Language focus

- Comparatives and superlatives
- *must / mustn't* and *should / shouldn't*

Unit aims

I can ...

- describe things in my house.
- compare things.
- understand information about different places to stay or live.
- talk about things I need to do and things which are a good idea to do.
- ask for and offer help.
- write a description of my dream house.

Vocabulary Things in the home

1 1.29 **Match the pictures with the words in the box and name the other things in the rooms. Then listen, check and repeat.**

carpet curtains pillow towel mirror wardrobe cupboard blanket shelf desk sink

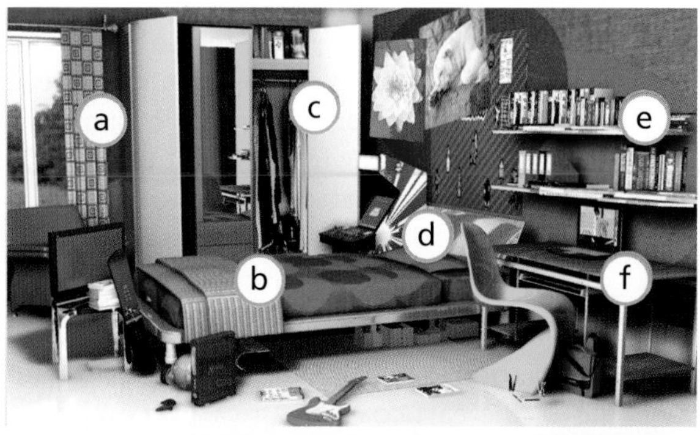

2 Look again at Exercise 1. Which ...

1 two things can you put on your bed?
2 two things do you put things in?
3 two things do you put things on?
4 thing do you close at night and open in the morning?
5 thing can you see yourself in?
6 thing do we put on the floor?

Your turn

3 Draw a plan of your bedroom. Include some of the things in Exercise 1.

4 Describe your bedroom to your partner. Your partner listens and draws it. Then swap.

In my bedroom, I've got a large bed in the middle of the room with two pillows and a green blanket.

Vocabulary bank • page 111

Reading An online forum

1 **Work with a partner. What's unusual about the hotels in the photos?**

2 1.30 **Read the online forum and check your ideas to Exercise 1. Then match the pictures to the posts (1–3).**

3 **Read the online forum again. Match the sentences with the hotels they describe.**

1 This hotel isn't in Europe. *Hotel 2*
2 This hotel closes in the summer.
3 A family stayed at this hotel.
4 You can't use a hairdryer at this hotel.
5 The hotel is nearest to the sea.
6 The temperature in the hotel is below zero.

Explore expressions with *do*

4 **Find two examples of *do* in the text. Which words follow them?**

5 **Make sentences about you and your family with *do* and the words in the box.**

housework the washing homework Maths sports the shopping

I did some housework on Saturday.

Vocabulary bank • page 111

Your turn

6 **Think of an idea for an unusual hotel. Write a short paragraph for the online forum. Talk about the things in the box.**

the place the view activities

We stayed in an unusual hotel. It was an old ship under the sea. My bedroom…

7 **Compare your ideas in groups. Then choose your favourite.**

THE MOST Unusual Hotels IN THE WORLD

There are many different hotels in the world; hotels for doing sports, city hotels or hotels for doing nothing. Last week, we asked you to tell us about the strangest hotels you know.

1 My parents stayed at the coldest hotel in the world – the Ice Hotel in Sweden. Open from December to April, it's the largest hotel made of snow and ice in the world. Their room was -5° C, but they said that the ice bed was more comfortable than their bed at home and the pillows were softer!

POSTED BY JACOB WILLIAMS 17:08 REPLY

2 When my cousin got married, she slept in the underwater room at a hotel on Pemba, one of the loveliest islands off the east coast of Africa. Every morning, they opened their curtains and saw the most beautiful fish in the world. They even swam with them!

POSTED BY LUCINDA THOMAS 15:59 REPLY

3 My family lives in the middle of Manchester. On holiday this year, we stayed at a treehouse hotel in a beautiful forest in Wales. It was much better than being in the city. Our bedrooms were high up in the trees. It was quieter and more relaxing and we did everything more slowly. But the worst thing? There wasn't any electricity so no TV!

POSTED BY NITA MEHTA 14:47 REPLY

a

b

c

FACT! *Capsule hotels began in Japan. The very small rooms or 'capsules' are big enough for a bed and nothing else so guests share a bathroom in the hall. The good thing is that they are cheaper than many other hotels.*

Language focus 1 Comparatives

1 Complete examples 1–4 from the text on page 42.

		Comparatives		Superlatives
short adjectives	soft	The pillows were [1]…. .	strange	Tell us about the [5]…. hotels in the world.
long adjectives	comfortable	The ice bed was [2]…. than their bed at home!	beautiful	… and saw the [6]…. fish in the world …
irregular adjectives	good	It was much [3]…. than being in the city.	bad	But the [7]…. thing?
adverbs	slowly	We did everything [4]…. .	quietly	I spoke **the most quietly**.

Grammar reference • page 103

Say it right! • page 96

2 Complete the sentences with the comparative form of the adjective or adverb in brackets.

1 London is …*smaller*… (small) than New York.
2 A holiday in the Amazon rainforest is …. (exciting) than a holiday in Paris.
3 I sleep …. (good) in my house than in a hotel.
4 My grandparents' house is …. (big) than my house.
5 I can study …. (easily) at school than at home.
6 My school canteen …. (noisy) than my classroom.

Superlatives

3 Complete examples 5–7 in the table above.

4 Write superlative sentences to complete the quiz. Then mark the sentences true (T) or false (F).

1 Russia / large / country in the world
2 Kilimanjaro / high / mountain in the world
3 Death Valley in California / hot / place in the world
4 The Atlantic / large / ocean in the world
5 The Vatican / small / country in the world
6 The cheetah / fast / animal in the world
7 The elephant / heavy / animal in the world

1 *Russia is the largest country in the world. T*

5 Choose the correct words.

Thousands of people visit Matmata in Tunisia every year. It's one of the [1]**more / most** popular places in this country because it's got some of the [2]**stranger / strangest** and also some of the [3]**older / oldest** homes in the world. Visitors can stay in a small underground hotel or in a [4]**larger / largest** modern hotel, which is [5]**more / most** expensive but less interesting. Why do so many people come here? Well, look at the photo [6]**more / most** carefully. Do you know it? They made the film *Star Wars* here!

6 Think about your dream hotel room. Make some notes. Then draw a picture.

7 Work with a partner. Describe and compare the pictures of your hotel rooms. Which is best?

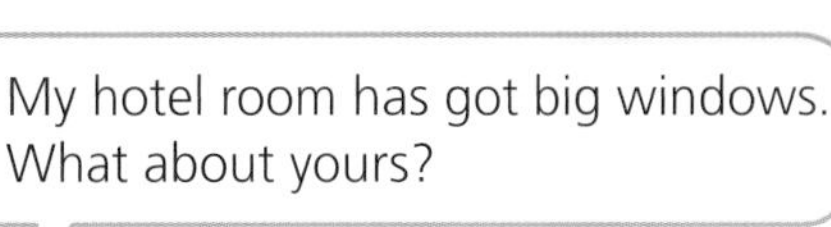

My hotel room has got big windows.
What about yours?

Learn about Joey and his Yukon log cabin.
- Why did Joey move out of his father's house?
- What was the problem with the log cabin?
- What did Joey decide to do with the cabin?

Listening An interview

1 **Theo is from the USA. Look at the photos. Where does he live? Do you think his life is easy?**

2 1.33 **Listen to the interview with Theo. Check your ideas to Exercise 1.**

3 1.33 **Listen again. Answer the questions.**

1. Where does Theo go to school?
2. What jobs does Theo do?
3. What does Theo's dad do in the circus?
4. When do they have circus training?
5. What does he say about his life at the end of the interview?

Vocabulary Household appliances

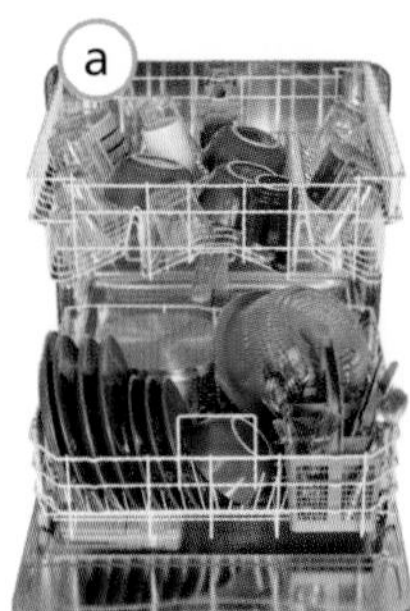

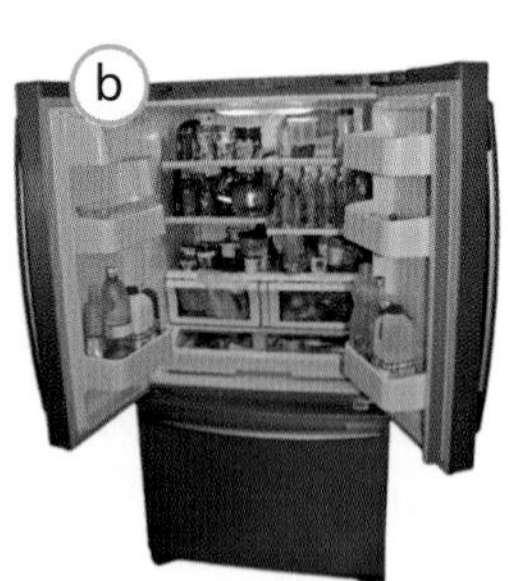

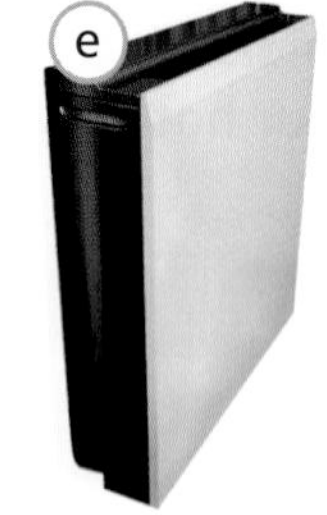

4 1.34 **Match the pictures with the words in the box. Then listen check and repeat.**

washing machine fridge heater lamp
cooker hairdryer freezer iron dishwasher

Your turn

5 **Write your answers to the questions.**

1. How often do you use the things in Exercise 4?
2. What housework do you usually do?
3. Do you think it's important for children to help their parents at home?

I use the dishwasher every day and I sometimes use the …

6 **Work with a partner. Ask and answer the questions in Exercise 5. Who helps more at home?**

How often do you use the dishwasher?

I use it every day. What about you?

Vocabulary bank • page 111

Language focus 2 *must/mustn't, should/shouldn't*

1 Complete the examples from the listening on page 44.

+	I [1]…. study a lot.
–	We [2]…. miss a class.

2 Look at the sentences in Exercise 1. Then complete the rules with *must* or *mustn't*.

We use [1]…. to say you need to do something.
We use [2]…. to say you can't do something.

Grammar reference • page 103

3 Choose the correct words.

1 You **must / mustn't** have a passport to go to the USA.
2 You **must / mustn't** go to school.
3 You **must / mustn't** use your mobile when you're driving.
4 You **must / mustn't** wear a seat belt in a car.
5 You **must / mustn't** leave a shop without paying.
6 You **must / mustn't** buy a ticket on a bus or train.

4 Complete the examples from the listening on page 44.

+	The teacher says I [1]…. work harder.
–	Some people say we [2]…. play with them.

5 Look at the sentences in Exercise 4. Then complete the rules with *should* or *shouldn't*.

We use [1]…. to say something is a good idea.
We use [2]…. to say something isn't a good idea.

Grammar reference • page 103

6 Complete the sentences with *should* or *shouldn't* and the verb in brackets.

1 You *shouldn't forget* (forget) your parents' birthday.
2 You …. (put) another blanket on your bed, if you're cold.
3 You …. (visit) my city. It's fantastic!
4 You …. (swim) in the sea today. It's dangerous.
5 You …. (help) your parents with housework.
6 You …. (do) more exercise if you want to get fit.
7 You …. (go) to bed late the day before an exam.

Get it right!

Use the infinitive without *to* after **must(n't)** and **should(n't)**:
You must ***tidy*** *your room before dinner.* ✓
~~*You must to tidy …*~~ ✗
You shouldn't ***watch*** *TV so late if you're tired.* ✓
~~*You shouldn't to watch …*~~ ✗

7 Complete the sentences about the UK with *must*, *mustn't*, *should* or *shouldn't*.

IN THE UK …

you [1] *must* be over 17 to drive a car.
you [2]…. buy a licence for your television.
you [3]…. say 'please' and 'thank you' as much as you can.
you [4]…. walk or sit on the grass in some parks.
you [5]…. give your seat to old people on a crowded bus or train.
you [6]…. take a present if someone invites you to their house.
you [7]…. open an umbrella inside the house.
you [8]…. call your teacher by his or her first name.

Your turn

8 Work with a partner. Write sentences with *must*, *mustn't*, *should* and *shouldn't* about the places in the box.

my house my school my sports centre my town the cinema

I must tidy my room before school. I must put my plate in the dishwasher. I should take off my shoes when I get home…

9 Work in small groups. Read your sentences from Exercise 8. Can the others guess the place?

I must tidy my room before school. I must put my plate in the dishwasher. I should take off my shoes when I get home …

Is it your house?

Yes, it is.

Discover Culture

1 Work with a partner. Look at the pictures. Ask and answer the questions.

1 Where do you think the people in Coober Pedy live?
2 What do you think the weather is like there?

2 4.2 Watch the video and check your answers to Exercise 1.

3 Test your memory. Which of the things below can you see in the video?

golf football cave mines swimming pool beach trucks diggers precious stones cactus bedroom factory

Find out about living in Coober Pedy.

4.2 A cool life

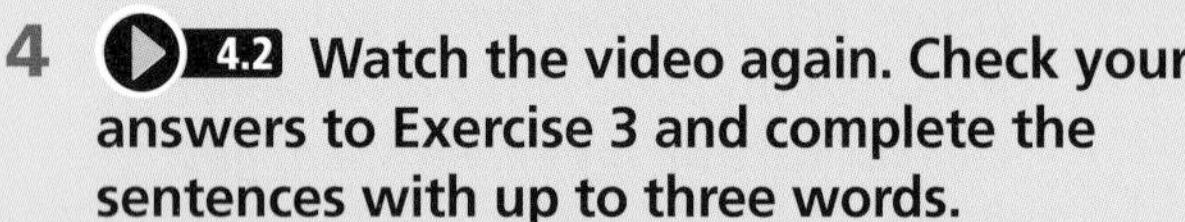

4 4.2 Watch the video again. Check your answers to Exercise 3 and complete the sentences with up to three words.

1 In summer, the temperature is between 35 °C and 45 °C.
2 Candice White and her husband live in an .... .
3 Inside the house, the temperature can be .... .
4 The population of Coober Pedy is only .... .
5 Most people came to Coober Pedy to look for .... .
6 So, everybody lives and works .... .

5 Test your memory. Mark the sentences true (*T*) or false (*F*). Correct the false ones.

1 Opals are black.
2 People wear lights on their heads to play golf.
3 People wear lights on their heads in the mines.
4 The golf ball is blue.
5 The golf course is in the middle of the desert.

Your turn

6 Compare living in your town in winter and in summer. Write sentences with the words in the box or your own ideas.

my house clothes sports food & drink free time

In winter, I've got more blankets on my bed.
In summer, I use a thinner blanket.

7 Work with a partner. Compare your sentences. Then decide if you prefer living in your town in the winter or in the summer.

In the winter, I've got more blankets on my bed. What about you?

Me too and I wear warmer clothes and gloves.

Reading A blog

1 **Look at the map and pictures. Where is Barrow? What do you think the weather is like there?**

2 **1.35 Read John's blog. Check your ideas to Exercise 1.**

3 **Read the blog again and choose the correct answer.**

1. Barrow is further north than **Greenland / Russia / any other town in the USA**.
2. In winter, the temperature's usually **higher than 0 °C / lower than 0 °C / 0 °C**.
3. In June, in Barrow it's **light / dark / rainy**.
4. John would like to **move somewhere warmer / stay in Barrow / change school**.
5. Nalukataq is **John's school / the spring / a festival**.

Explore verbs with *up* or *down*

4 **Look at the blog again. Find two verbs with *up* or *down*. What do they mean?**

5 **Complete the sentences with the verb in brackets and *up* or *down*.**

1. The sun didn't *come up* until 7.30 this morning. (come)
2. If you know the answer, you should .... your hand. (put)
3. I'm tired. I want to .... on my bed. (lie)
4. Visitors often .... that hill because they can see the whole city from the top. (go)
5. Why are you sitting on top of the wardrobe? .... now! It's dangerous. (come)

Vocabulary bank • page 111

Your turn

6 **What are the best and worst things about living in your town? Write sentences with the words in the box or your own ideas.**

weather people food and drink free-time activities noise

One of the best things is the weather. It's warm and sunny in the summer.

7 **Work in small groups. Would you prefer to live in your town or somewhere else? Use your ideas from Exercise 6.**

Living in Barrow, Alaska

Barrow

I'm John, from Barrow in Alaska, which is the most northern town in the USA. So what's it like living here? Well, in November, the sun goes down and it doesn't come up again until January. That means it's dark for 65 days. Of course, these are the coldest months of the year, even the highest temperature is below zero! It's also the most boring time of the year, we can't go out without our parents because it's too dark. Summer is better. In May, the sun stays up so there's no night for 85 days.

Why don't we move somewhere warmer? We love living here. I know everyone in the town, I love the school and we've got some amazing traditions and festivals. The best is Nalukataq in the spring when the fishermen return to our town with whale meat. Then, we make a special blanket. It's huge. A dancer stands in the middle of the blanket and we throw him or her into the air. When the dancer is in the air, they throw sweets to the children. It's fantastic – you should come and join us next year!

FACT! *The coldest inhabited place on Earth is Oymyakon in North East Russia. On 6 February 1933, it was –67.7 °C. That's freezing!*

Speaking Asking for and offering help

Real talk: Which do you prefer – houses or flats?

1 **4.3 Watch the teenagers in the video. Do they prefer flats (*F*), houses (*H*) or both (*B*)? Why?**

a) Speaker 1 *H bigger, more space*
b) Speaker 2
c) Speaker 3
d) Speaker 4
e) Speaker 5
f) Speaker 6

2 **Work with your partner. Which do *you* prefer – houses or flats?**

3 **1.36 Listen to Josh and his dad talking about housework. Which jobs does Josh agree to do?**

4 **1.36 Complete the conversation with the useful language. Then listen and check your answers.**

Useful language

Can you give me a hand?
I'll do it.
Can you do me a favour?
Yes, of course.
Shall I ...?
I'll give you a hand.

Dad: Josh, dinner's nearly ready! [1]....
Josh: Yes. [2].... **lay the table**?
Dad: Thanks! [3].... Could you **take the dog for a walk** after dinner as well?
Josh: Sorry, Dad, I can't! **I've got a lot of homework to do**.
Dad: You always say that!
Josh: It's true! Anyway, it's **Hayley's** turn. Shall I ask her?
Dad: That's OK. [4]....
Josh: OK. After dinner [5].... to **put the plates in the dishwasher**, but then I need to finish an essay.
Dad: OK. And can you go and tell **Hayley** it's dinnertime, please?
Josh: [6]....

5 **Work with a partner. Practise the conversation in Exercise 4.**

6 **Work with a partner. Change the words in bold in the conversation in Exercise 4. Use the ideas below or your own. Then practise the conversation.**

do the washing clean the microwave
tidy your room wash up

Writing A description of a house

1 Look at the picture and read Kevin's description of his dream house. Would you like to live there?

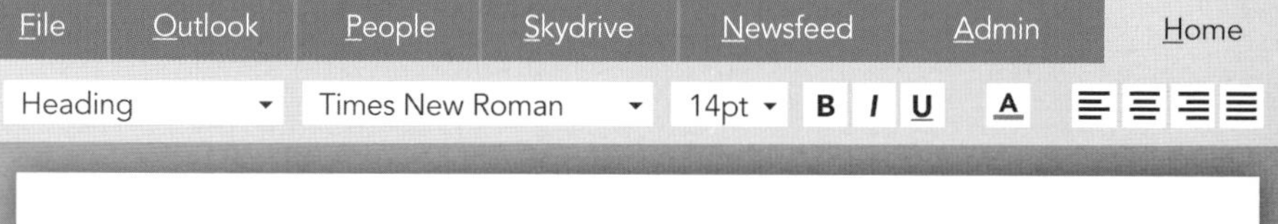

My dream home is a large modern house in the city centre. It's got two floors and a lift. Downstairs there's a living room with the biggest TV in the world. There's also a swimming pool and a tennis court.

My bedroom's upstairs with its own bathroom. There's a jacuzzi in the bathroom and a huge brown bed in the middle of the bedroom with lots of pillows. Next to it, there's a machine for making fresh juice in the morning. There's a large window above my bed so I can see the whole city from here when the curtains are open.

You should come and visit me soon!

2 Read Kevin's description again and answer the questions.

1 Is Kevin's dream home a flat or a house?
2 Where is it?
3 Where's Kevin's bedroom? What's it like?
4 What can Kevin do in his bedroom?

3 Look at the Useful language box. Find examples of adjectives in Kevin's description.

Useful language

Order of adjectives

When we use two or more adjectives together, we use this order:

- *I've got a **brilliant new** computer.*
- *My mum bought me a **big red** towel for the beach.*
- *There's an **amazing purple** picture on the wall.*

4 Complete the table with the words in the box.

small old green and yellow beautiful

Opinion	Fact			Noun
	Size	Age	Colour	
fantastic	*large*	*new*	*blue*	blanket
1	2	3	4	towel

5 Rewrite the sentences with the adjectives in brackets.

1 I've got a wardrobe. (old, large) *I've got a large old wardrobe.*
2 I'm sitting in my kitchen. (white, modern)
3 My grandparents have got a sofa in their living room. (red, comfortable)
4 We've got a fridge. (huge, silver)
5 There was a carpet on the floor. (red and black, strange)
6 I'd like to buy a laptop. (smaller, more modern)

PLAN

6 Make notes about your dream home. Use the questions in Exercise 2.

WRITE

7 Write a description of your dream home. Use your notes from Exercise 6, and the language below.

My dream home is …
It's got … and ….
Downstairs there's a … with …
There's also a …
Next to it, there's a …
You should come and visit me soon.

CHECK

8 Can you say YES to these questions?

- Have you got adjectives to describe the things in your home?
- Have you got the information from Exercise 6?
- Have you got the language from Exercise 7?

3–4 Review

Vocabulary

1 Match the sentence halves.

1 The thief climbed …
2 He jumped …
3 The police officer chased …
4 The police officer didn't …
5 The thief hid …
6 The thief threw …

a behind a tree.
b a tree.
c his bag into the river.
d into the garden.
e the thief for 2 km.
f catch the thief.

2 Complete the sentences with the adverbial form of the words in the box.

happy careful easy quick quiet slow

1 It's getting late. Please finish your work .... .
2 Please talk .... in the library.
3 The exam wasn't difficult. I passed it .... .
4 We're really late! You're walking very .... .
5 Your little brother isn't sad. He's .... eating an ice cream over there.
6 Those books are very old! Please look at them .... .

3 Read the descriptions of some things in the home. What is the word?

1 You put your clothes in this. w _ _ _ _ _ _ _
2 People use this to look at themselves. m _ _ _ _ _
3 This is something you put on your bed to feel warmer. b _ _ _ _ _ _
4 Students sit at this type of table to study. d _ _ _
5 You need this to dry yourself after a shower. t _ _ _ _
6 People wash dirty things in this. s _ _ _

4 Match the household appliances with the pictures.

freezer hairdryer washing machine cooker dishwasher

Explore vocabulary

5 Choose the correct answers.

1 I wanted to ask a question so I put **up / off** my hand.
2 My sister couldn't find her keys so I helped her look **for / at** them.
3 I was feeling ill so I went to lie **on / down**.
4 Your brother looks **for / like** a rock star with his long hair.
5 Could you look **after / up** my dog while I buy some milk?

6 Complete the sentences with the name of the person. Look at the words in bold to help you.

1 My brother takes a lot of **photographs**. He's an amazing *photographer* .
2 We visited the **island** of Malta last summer. The .... were very friendly.
3 My friend Julia **swims** very quickly. She's a champion .... .
4 My dad **builds** houses all week. He works as a .... .
5 My cousins live on a **farm** because their dad is a .... .
6 Marco Polo **explored** China. He was a famous .... .

7 Complete the sentences with *do* and the words in the box.

homework the shopping Maths housework sports the washing

1 Can you buy some biscuits when you ...., please?
2 I sometimes .... at home. I tidy my bedroom and I empty the bins.
3 I have no clean clothes. I need to .... .
4 On Monday morning at school, we ...., and then Geography and English.
5 At school, we .... a lot of .... . My favourite one is tennis.
6 I often .... my .... in the library because it's very quiet there.

Language focus

1 Complete the questions and answers with the past continuous. Use the information in the table.

yesterday	Maria	Robert
10 am	play tennis	swim
12 noon	study with Robert	study with Maria

1 A: What [1].... Maria .... at 10 am yesterday?
  B: She [2].... tennis.
2 A: [3].... Robert .... tennis at 10 am yesterday?
  B: [4]...., he .... . He [5].... .
3 A: What [6].... Maria and Robert .... at 12 noon?
  B: They [7].... .

2 Write sentences using the past simple and past continuous.

1 He / answer / the phone / while / he / eat
  He answered the phone while he was eating.
2 We / have / a picnic / when / it / start to rain
3 Tara / break / her glasses / while / she / play tennis
4 I / read / a magazine / when / the window / break
5 The film / start / while / they / buy / tickets

3 Write sentences with *could/couldn't*.

	six years old	seven years old	ten years old
Marta	(1) count in English (✗)	(3) ride a skateboard (✓)	(5) play the violin (✓)
Sam	(2) swim ten metres (✓)	(4) use a computer (✗)	(6) make a cake (✗)

1 *Marta couldn't count in English when she was six.*

4 Write sentences with *be* and the comparative form of the adjectives.

1 Our new house / big / our old house
2 This small hotel / comfortable / a large hotel
3 These laptops / good / desktop computers
4 My class / noisy / your class
5 Your friends / interesting / my friends

5 Complete the sentences with the superlative form of the adjectives in brackets.

1 Burj Khalifa in Dubai is .... (tall) building in the world.
2 Mawsynram in India is .... (wet) place in the world.
3 Kilauea in Hawaii is .... (active) volcano in the world.
4 The cheetah is .... (fast) animal in the world.
5 Commonwealth Bay in Antarctica is .... (windy) place in the world.

6 Look at the sign. Then choose the correct answers.

Computer room rules

No food!
No computer games!
Don't use printers!
Please talk quietly.
Please ask for help.

1 You **mustn't / should** bring food into the room.
2 You **mustn't / shouldn't** play computer games.
3 You **should / shouldn't** talk loudly to your friends.
4 You **must / should** ask for help.
5 You **mustn't / shouldn't** use the printers.

Language builder

7 Choose the correct answers.

Kara: I [1].... at my new school [2].... week.
Jenny: How is it? Is it the [3].... school in the city?
Kara: I'm not sure about that but it's [4].... my house so now I've got [5].... for breakfast.
Jenny: Cool! [6].... you make friends on the first day?
Kara: Yes, of course. I also learned the rules. We mustn't [7].... inside and we [8].... switch off our mobile phones.

1 a start — b started
2 a past — b last
3 a better — b best
4 a near — b nearer
5 a enough time — b time enough
6 a Was — b Did
7 a run — b to run
8 a mustn't — b must

Speaking

8 Complete the conversations with the words in the box.

How Can you give me Yes, of course Shall I Something strange happened What?

Liz: [1].... this morning.
Pete: Really? [2].... ?
Liz: A family of mice fell down our chimney and got into the living room!
Pete: [3].... weird!

Luke: These bags are heavy. [4].... a hand?
Jenny: [5].... . [6].... take the green bag?
Luke: Thanks.

Unit 1 /f/

The final sound in *enough* is pronounced /f/.

1 1.08 **Listen and repeat.**

/f/ enough

2 **Which of the following words also have this sound?**

of laugh elephant through
coffee phone off

3 1.09 **Listen and check.**

4 **Write down ten more words that have the sound /f/.**

5 **How many ways can you spell the sound /f/?**

Unit 2 Irregular verbs

1 1.16 **Listen and repeat the irregular past simple verbs.**

read thought came had drank left
ate saw sat gave taught said

2 **Put the verbs in the correct column.**

/e/ **red**	/ɔ:/ **four**	/æ/ **cat**	/ei/ **train**
read, …			

3 1.17 **Listen and check your answers.**

4 **Work with a partner. Talk about what you did yesterday. Use the irregular verbs above.**

Yesterday morning, I saw my friends at school. In the evening, I ate dinner with my parents, and then I read my book.

Unit 3 *was/were*

1 1.24 **Listen to the questions and answers. How do we say *was* and *were*?**

Detective:	What were you doing between 8 and 8.30 last night?
Schoolboy:	I was looking at my Maths book.
Detective:	Why were you studying Maths?
Schoolboy:	Because I've got an exam tomorrow.
Detective:	Where were you sitting?
Schoolboy:	In my bedroom.
Detective:	Were you talking to anyone at the same time?
Schoolboy:	No, I was doing it alone.

2 1.24 **Listen and repeat the dialogue.**

3 **Work with a partner. Practise the dialogue.**

Unit 4 *schwa*

1 1.31 **Listen to the sentences. How do we pronounce the letters in bold?**

1 France is small**er** th**a**n Brazil.
2 I'm bett**er** **a**t Maths th**a**n **a**t History.
3 This classroom is bigg**er** th**a**n our classroom last year.

2 1.31 **Listen again and repeat the sentences.**

3 **Underline the *schwa* sounds in the following sentences.**

1 Mark is older than Julia, but Peter is the oldest in the class.
2 The River Nile is longer than the River Danube.
3 The weather is warmer in Spain than in England.

4 1.32 **Listen and check your answers.**

This page is intentionally left blank

Grammar reference

Starter Unit

Subject pronouns and *be*

+	I	am	13 years old.
	He / She / It	is	
	You / We / They	are	
–	I	'm not	from Manchester.
	He / She / It	isn't	
	You / We / They	aren't	
?	Am	I	in a sports team?
	Is	he / she / it	
	Are	you / we / they	

+	Yes,	I	am.
		he / she / it	is.
		you / we / they	are.
–	No,	I	'm not.
		he / she / it	isn't.
		you / we / they	aren't.

- *I, you, he, she, it, we*, and *they* are subject pronouns. We use them before the verb to say who does the action:
  I'm Nathan and I'm from Newcastle.
- We use *be* to describe people and things, say how old they are, where they are, where they are from etc:
  I'm John. I'm 14 years old. I'm from Scotland.

1 Write complete questions with *be*. Then write true answers for you. Use subject pronouns in your answers.

1 How old / you?
How old are you? I'm 13 years old.
2 your best friend / in your class?
3 Where / your friends?
4 your pencil case / on your desk?
5 When / your next Maths class?
6 you and your friends / from Colombia?

Possessive *'s*

singular	My brother's name is Matt.
plural	My friends' names are Kate, Lucy and Natalie.

- We use the possessive *'s* to talk about our things or possessions:
  My sister's bike, my dad's car, etc (NOT the bike of my sister).
- With a plural noun, we write the apostrophe (') after the *s*:
  My friends' phones, my cousins' dog etc.

2 Write one sentence with possessive *'s*.

1 My sister's got a bike. It's blue.
My sister's bike is blue.
2 My best friend's got a dog. It's very big.
3 My parents have got a car. It's new.
4 I've got three cousins. Their names are Jack, Will and Frances.
5 My teacher has got two cats. They're black.
6 My friends have got skateboards. They're under their desks.

there is/are, some/any

	singular	plural
+	There's some food on the floor.	There are some posters on the walls.
–	There isn't any milk on the table.	There aren't any students in the canteen.
?	Is there any water in your glass?	Are there any balls outside?

+	Yes, there is.	Yes, there are.
–	No, there isn't.	No, there aren't.

- We use *there is / are* to say something exists (or doesn't exist):
  There's a computer in my bedroom but there isn't a TV.
- We use *there is* with singular and uncountable nouns:
  There's a dog in the park.
- We use *there are* with plural countable nouns:
  There are 10 laptops in the IT room.
- We often use *there is / are* with *some* in affirmative sentences:
  There's some orange juice for you.
- We often use *there is / are* with *any* in negative sentences and questions:
  Are there any books on the floor?

3 Circle the correct words and then write *some* or *any*.

1 A *Is there / Are there* .... pencils under your desk?
B No, *there isn't / there aren't* but *there is / there are* .... rubbers.
2 A *There isn't / There aren't* .... English dictionaries in the classroom.
B Yes, I know but *there is / there are* two big dictionaries in the library.
3 A *Is there / Are there* .... orange juice?
B No, *there isn't / there aren't* but *there is / there are* .... cola.
4 A *Is there / Are there* an IT room in your school?
B No, *there isn't / there aren't* but *there is / there are* .... laptops in all the classrooms.

Grammar reference

have got

+	I / You / We / They	have got	an apple.
	He / She / It	has got	
–	I / You / We / They	haven't got	any cousins.
	He / She / It	hasn't got	
?	Have	I / you / we / they	a dog?
	Has	he / she / it	

+	Yes,	I / you / we / they	have.
		he / she / it	has.
–	No,	I / you / we / they	haven't.
		he / she / it	hasn't.

- We use *have / has got* to talk about our family, our hair or eyes and our possessions:
  I've got a sister. She's got brown hair and blue eyes.

4 Complete the sentences with *has got, have got, hasn't* got or *haven't got.*

1 I .... (✗) a big family. I .... (✓) a brother, a mum and a dad.
2 My mum .... (✓) three brothers but she .... (✗) any sisters.
3 .... you .... a rubber in your pencil case?
4 My best friend .... (✗) a skateboard but he .... (✓) a new mountain bike.
5 My friends .... (✓) PE now but I .... (✓) Maths.
6 What .... the teacher .... in that big bag?

Present simple: affirmative and negative

+	I / You / We / They	play	basketball.
	He / She / It	plays	
–	I / You / We / They	don't go	swimming.
	He / She / It	doesn't go	

- We use the present simple to talk about facts, habits and routines:
  I play football after school every day.

Spelling: third person

- With most verbs, we add *-s*:
  play – he plays   *live – he lives*
- With verbs that end in consonant + *-y*, remove the *-y* and add *-ies*:
  study – she studies   *fly – it flies*
- With verbs that end *in -o, -ss, -sh, -ch, -x* and *-zz*, add *-es:*
  does   misses   washes   watches
  relaxes   buzzes

5 Write sentences in the present simple.

1 In winter, I (✗ go skiing / ✓ go snowboarding).
In winter, I don't go skiing. I go snowboarding.
2 My mum (✓ have lunch at work / ✗ have lunch at home).
3 My cousins (✗ live near me / ✓ live in Glasgow).
4 My best friend (✓ do his homework / ✗ watch TV).
5 My brother (✗ study French / ✓ study English).

Present simple: questions

?	Do	I / you / we / they	play	volleyball?
	Does	he / she / it		

+	Yes,	I / you / we / they	do.
		he / she / it	does.
–	No,	I / you / we / they	don't.
		he / she / it	doesn't.

6 Write questions in the present simple.

1 **A:** .... you .... basketball?
B: No, I don't. I play football.
2 **A:** How often .... your sister .... swimming?
B: She goes swimming every day.
3 **A:** .... your parents .... TV after dinner?
B: Yes, they do. They always watch TV after dinner.
4 **A:** Where .... your best friend .... ?
B: She lives near me.
5 **A:** When .... you and your friends .... skateboarding?
B: We go skateboarding at the weekend.

Adverbs of frequency

always 100%   usually   often   sometimes   never 0%

- We use the present simple with **adverbs of frequency** to say how often we do things.
  I sometimes go snowboarding in the winter.
- With the verb ***be***, we put the adverb after the verb:
  I'm often tired after playing football.
- With other verbs in the present simple, we put the adverb before the main verb:
  I sometimes go cycling with my friends.

7 Put the words in order to make sentences.

1 library / the / We / do / in / sometimes / English
2 work / dad / often / cycling / after / goes / My
3 always / is / brother / happy / My
4 lunch / canteen / usually / have / I / the / in
5 grandparents / never / skiing / My / go

Grammar reference

Unit 1

Present continuous

+	I	am	eating.
	He / She / It	is	
	You / We / They	are	
–	I	am not	
	He / She / It	isn't	
	You / We / They	aren't	
?	Am	I	eating?
	Is	he / she / it	
	Are	you / we / they	

+	Yes,	I	am.
		he / she / it	is.
		you / we / they	are.
–	No,	I	am not.
		he / she / it	isn't.
		you / we / they	aren't.

- We use the present continuous to talk about actions in progress at the time of speaking.
  You're reading the Grammar reference.

1 Complete the sentences with the present continuous form of the verb in brackets.

1 I .... (visit) an amazing shopping centre right now.
2 We .... (study) in the library today.
3 I can see Martha. She .... (not play) tennis. It's badminton.
4 What film .... you .... (watch) on TV? Is it good?
5 My parents are in the kitchen but they .... (not cook).
6 .... your friends .... (shop) in town at the moment? Yes, they .... .

Present simple vs. present continuous

- We use the present simple to talk about facts, habits and routines. We use adverbs of frequency with the present simple.
  I never go to the cinema.
- We use the present continuous to talk about actions in progress at the time of speaking. We use *at the moment* and *(right) now* with the present continuous.
  I am reading my emails at the moment.

2 Choose the correct words.

1 Paula **look / looks / is looking / are looking** at trainers in a sports shop right now.
2 Dan and Eddie **play / plays / is playing / are playing** rugby on Saturdays.
3 Where **do / does / am / are** you usually **go / goes / going / to go** after class?
4 **Do / Does / Is / Are** she **buy / buys / buying / to buy** a tablet right now?
5 We **eat / eats / am eating / are eating** at the shopping mall now.

(don't) want to, would(n't) like to, would prefer to

- *Would like* is more polite than *want*.
  I want to have pizza for dinner, please. (= child to parent)
  I'd like to have some chips with my fish, please. (= customer to waiter).
- We use *would prefer* to say what we want to do in a situation (not in general).
  I would prefer to buy my new trainers in the sports shop.
- We use the infinitive with *to* after *want*, *would like* and *would prefer*.
  She'd like to see the new shopping centre.

3 Write sentences or questions.

1 I / would like / visit / the zoo
2 My brother / not want / go / to the theme park
3 We / would prefer / watch / a funny film
4 your cousin / want / sell / his old games console?
5 My friends / not would like / live / in another town
6 Would like / you / have / dinner with us?

(not) enough + noun

- We use *enough* + noun to say we've got what we need or want.
  I can buy a new mobile phone. I've got enough money.
- We use *not enough* + noun to say we've got less than we need or want.
  I can't buy a new phone. I haven't got enough money.
- *Enough* goes before the noun.
  We can't make a cake. There isn't enough milk.

4 Order the words to make sentences.

1 money / tablet / enough / haven't / for / a / I / got
2 you / got / time / help / enough / Have / me / to / ?
3 are / enough / for / There / oranges / orange juice
4 enough / We / got / haven't / for / chairs / everyone
5 car / Our / enough / isn't / six / people / for / big

Grammar reference

Unit 2

was/were: affirmative and negative

+	I / He / She / It	was	calm.
	You / We / They	were	
–	I/ He / She / It	wasn't	
	You / We / They	weren't	

Was and *were* are the past simple forms of *be*.
He was a tennis player. They weren't actors.

1 Complete the sentences with *was, were, wasn't* or *weren't*.

1 My friends .... tired after the match.
2 You .... late for school yesterday.
3 We .... (not) in class at 7 o'clock.
4 I .... born in 2002.
5 Nelson Mandela .... (not) from England.
6 It .... (not) cold last night.

Past simple: affirmative, negative and time expressions

+	I / You / He / She / It / We / They	watched TV last night.
–		didn't play tennis on Thursday.

- We use the past simple to talk about completed events and actions in the past.
  We played basketball yesterday.
- We often use time expressions such as *yesterday, last week, at 6 o'clock, in 2007, on Monday,* etc. with the past simple to say when the action happened.
  My parents weren't at work at 6 o'clock.

Past Simple: spelling

- For verbs ending in *-e*, we add *-d*.
  like – liked   live – lived
- For verbs ending in consonant + *-y*, we remove the *-y* and add *-ied*.
  copy – copied   study – studied   bully – bullied
- For verbs ending in consonant + vowel + consonant, we double the last consonant and add *-ed*.
  shop – shopped   stop – stopped
  travel – travelled
- Some verbs are irregular in the past simple. They don't follow any pattern.
- See the irregular verb list on p127.

2 Write sentences in the past simple.

1 Marie Curie / live / in Paris.
2 My dad / fly / to New York five days ago.
3 My friends / not play / football in the morning.
4 I / win / a race at school yesterday.
5 We / not buy / anything at the shopping centre on Saturday.
6 My sister / find / some money on the floor.

was/were: questions and short answers

?	Was	I / he / she / it	friendly?
	Were	you / we / they	

+	Yes,	I / he / she / it	was.
		you / we / they	were.
–	No,	I / he / she / it	wasn't.
		you / we / they	weren't.

3 Write questions with the past simple of the verb *be*.

1 Where / she / born?
2 What / her first film?
3 What / her favourite subjects at school?
4 you / interested in acting / at school?
5 your father / a film director?
6 your parents / interested in films?

Past simple: questions and short answers

?	Did	I / you / he / she / it / we / they	sleep?

+	Yes,	I / you / he / she / it / we / they	did.
–	No,		didn't.

4 Read the answers and write questions in the past simple.

1 A: Where .... last night?
  B: I went to the cinema.
2 A: Who .... at the restaurant?
  B: I saw a famous actor.
3 A: When .... on holiday?
  B: My parents went on holiday a week ago.
4 A: .... at the concert last night?
  B: No, I wasn't at the concert. I was at home.
5 A: .... for the exam after school?
  B: Yes, I did. I studied for two hours.
6 A: Why .... about your grandmother?
  B: I wrote about her because I admire her.

Grammar reference

Unit 3

Past continuous: affirmative and negative

+	I / He / She / It	was	eating.
	You / We / They	were	
–	I / He / She / It	wasn't	
	You / We / They	weren't	

- We use the past continuous to talk about a long action in progress at a certain time in the past.
At midday, I was having lunch with my friend.

1 Write sentences in the past continuous.

At 5 o'clock yesterday afternoon ...

1 My teacher (✗ read / ✓ talk to a friend).
My teacher wasn't reading. She was talking to a friend.
2 The dog (✗ sleep / ✓ run in the garden).
3 I (✗ write a letter / ✓ read an email).
4 The children (✗ watch TV / ✓ do homework).
5 You (✗ study / ✓ play computer games).
6 It (✗ rain / ✓ snow).

Past continuous: questions and short answers

?	Were	you / they / we	walking?
	Was	he / she / it / I	

+	Yes,	you / they / we	were.
		he / she / it / I	was.
–	No,	you / they / we	weren't
		he / she / it / I	wasn't.

2 Complete the questions and answers with the past continuous.

1 A: What .... you .... (do) last night?
B: I .... (listen) to music, but I .... (not listen) to it loudly.
2 A: .... Rachel .... (watch) a film this afternoon?
B: No, she .... . She .... (tidy) her bedroom.
3 A: Where .... they .... (chase) the dog?
B: They .... (chase) it in the park, but they .... (not run) very fast.
4 A: .... you .... (study) for the Science test yesterday?
B: Yes, I .... . I .... (work) with Ben.

Past simple vs. continuous

- We use the past continuous to talk about a long action that was in progress in the past. We use the past simple to talk about a short action that interrupts another long action. We usually use *when* before the past simple and *while* before the past continuous.
I was talking to my mum when I heard the news.

3 Complete the sentences with the past simple or past continuous form of the verb in brackets.

1 I .... (break) my arm while I .... (climb) a tree.
2 Dan .... (do) a Maths test, when his phone .... (ring).
3 The police .... (catch) the thief while he .... (jump) over the wall.
4 When my mum .... (get) home, we .... (not do) our homework.
5 While I .... (take) photos in the town centre, I .... (see) my best friend.
6 My friends .... (swim) in the sea when it .... (start) to rain.

could/couldn't: affirmative, negative, questions and short answers

+	I / You / He / She / It / We / They	could	swim very well.
–		couldn't	

?	Could	I / you / he / she / it / we / they	swim very well?

+	Yes,	I / you / he / she / it / we / they	could.
–	No,		couldn't.

- We use *could/couldn't* to talk about ability and possibility in the past.
When I was five, I could swim 20 metres.

4 Complete the sentences with *could(n't)* and the verb in brackets.

1 I .... when I was five. (read)
2 She .... very fast because she was tired. (not run)
3 Sam .... the board because he wasn't wearing his glasses. (not see)
4 .... the piano when he was small? (Tony, play)
5 We .... him because he spoke slowly. (understand)
6 .... a bike when you were a child? (you, ride)

Grammar reference

Unit 4

Comparatives and superlatives

	Adjective	Comparative	Superlative
Short adjectives	high	add *-er*: *higher*	add *-est*: *the highest*
Short adjectives ending vowel + consonant	big	double the final consonant and add *-er*: *bigger*	double the final consonant and add *-est*: *the biggest*
Adjectives ending *-y*	tidy	remove the *-y* and add *-ier*: *tidier*	remove the *-y* and add *-iest*: *the tidiest*
Long adjectives	comfortable	*more comfortable*	*the most comfortable*
Irregular adjectives	good	*better*	*the best*

- We use comparative adjectives to compare one thing with another. Use the verb + a comparative adjective + *than*.
  My room is tidier than my sister's room.
- We use superlative adjectives to say that one thing or person has got the most of a particular quality. Use *the* with a superlative adjective.
  My parents have got the biggest bedroom.

1 Complete the sentences with the comparative or superlative form of the adjective or adverb.

1 My bedroom is .... my sister's room. (small)
2 We stayed at .... hotel in the city. (bad)
3 I run .... my brother. (fast)
4 We all eat fast in my family, but my older brother eats .... . (quickly)
5 Scott is .... player on the team. (good)
6 I think doing housework is .... doing homework. (boring)

must and *mustn't*

+	I / You / He / She / It / We / They	must	speak.
–		mustn't	

- We use *must* to talk about obligation or strong recommendations.
  We must do our homework.
- We use *mustn't* to talk about prohibition and strong advice against something.
  They mustn't talk in the cinema.

2 Complete the sentences with *must* or *mustn't* and the verb in brackets.

1 Children .... (go) to school.
2 You .... (wear) a helmet when you ride a motorbike.
3 You .... (swim) on a beach when the flag is red.
4 You .... (talk) in a library.
5 When the traffic lights are red, you .... (stop).
6 You .... (forget) your passport when you travel to another country.

should and *shouldn't*

+	I / You / He / She / It / We / They	should	be quiet.
–		shouldn't	

?	Should	I / you / he / she / it / we / they	go out?

+	Yes,	I / you / he / she / it / we / they	should.
–	No,		shouldn't.

- We use *should* and *shouldn't* when we give advice or recommendations.
  You should study for the exam.

3 Complete the questions with *should* and the words in brackets. Then answer the questions.

1 A: I'm bored. Who *should I phone* ? (I / phone)
B: *You should phone a friend. You shouldn't phone your teacher.*
2 A: We're hungry but lunch is in 30 minutes. What .... ? (we / eat)
B: ....
3 A: My brother's got an exam tomorrow. What time .... ? (he / go to bed)
B: ....
4 A: I would like to visit your town. When .... ? (I / visit)
B: ....
5 A: My friends want to try a new sport. What .... ? (they / try)
B: ....
6 A: My sister wants to learn French. Where .... ? (she / go)
B: ....

Vocabulary Bank

Jog your memory!

1 **Cover the rest of the page. How many shops and money verbs can you remember?**

Shops

bookshop	electronics shop	shoe shop
chemist	music shop	sports shop
clothes shop	newsagent	supermarket
department store		

1 **Think of two things you can buy from each shop in the box.**
bookshop – magazine, dictionary

2 **Work with a partner. Say two things you can buy in one of the shops. Your partner says the shop. Then swap.**

Money verbs

spend buy sell borrow save earn

1 **Which four verbs in the box often go with the word *money*? Which two verbs often go with things like *clothes, shoes, books,* etc.?**

2 **Write true sentences about you with the words.**
1 I sometimes spend money in the music shop.

Explore *extreme adjectives*

~~amazing~~	brilliant	huge	terrible
awful	freezing	horrible	wonderful
boiling	great		

1 **Complete the table with the words in the box.**

very good	very bad	other
amazing		

2 **Work with a partner. Decide together on things which are *amazing, awful, brilliant,* etc.**
The Dubai shopping mall is amazing.

Explore prefixes

afraid	happy	lucky	usual
clear	important	tidy	well
friendly	interesting		

1 **What do we add to the adjectives in the box to make the negative?**

2 **Work with a partner. Think of a situation for six of the negative adjectives.**
When you are ill, you feel unwell.

Study tip

Shops and money
bookshop (n)

Start a vocabulary notebook or make some vocabulary cards. Keep a record of all your new words. Write the heading '*Shops and money*' and write the words on this page under this heading. Don't forget to write the part of speech next to the new word, e.g. *noun*, *verb* or *adjective*.

Vocabulary Bank

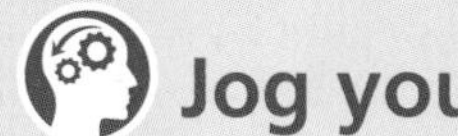

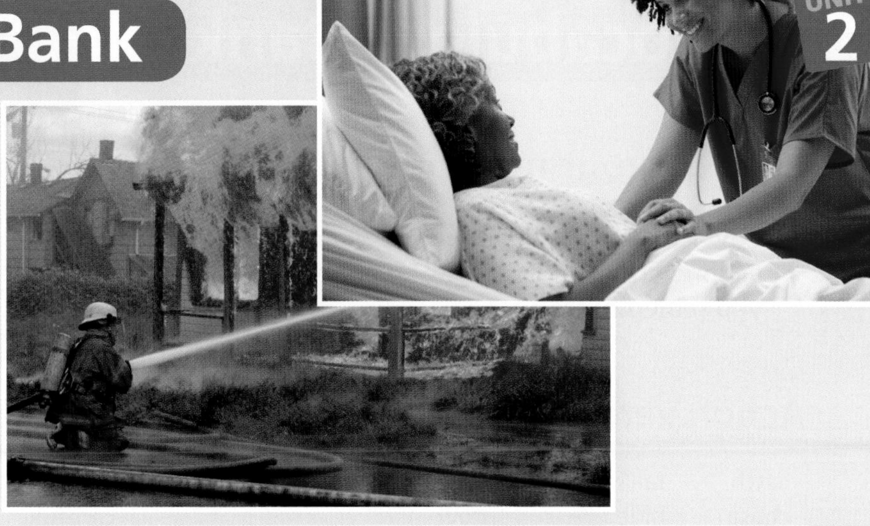

Jog your memory!

1 **Cover the rest of the page. How many jobs and adjectives of character can you remember?**

Jobs

actor	firefighter	scientist
artist	police officer	vet
astronaut	musician	
dancer	nurse	

1 **Look at the words in the box. What do the people do?**
An actor acts in films or plays.

2 **Work with a partner. Say what one of the people does. Your partner says the job. Then swap.**

Adjectives of character

brave	friendly	quiet
calm	funny	serious
cheerful	kind	

1 **Match the words in the box with some of the jobs on this page and write a sentence. Compare your sentences with a partner.**
An actor needs to be brave and funny.

Explore expressions with *make*

a bed	history	a suggestion
a cake	mistakes	sure
friends	a phone call	

1 **Look at the words in the box for one minute. Cover them. How many can you remember?**

2 **Work with a partner. Write true/false sentences about you with the phrases.**
Yesterday, I made a cake.

3 **Tell your partner your sentences. He/She must guess if they are true or false.**

Explore the suffix *-ness*

friendly	kind	tidy
happy	quiet	weak
ill	sad	

1 **Look at the words in the box. What do we add to these adjectives to make nouns? Write down the nouns but check your spelling!**

2 **Work with a partner. Say the noun. Your partner makes a sentence with the adjective. Then swap.**

Study tip

Write a short definition of the words in your vocabulary notebook or on the cards. This will help you to remember the meaning. When you study these words later, cover the word, read your definition and try to remember the word.

Actor – an actor acts in films and plays.

Vocabulary Bank

Jog your memory!

1 **Cover the rest of the page. How many action verbs and adverbs of manner can you remember?**

Action verbs

catch	fall over	run
chase	hide	throw
climb	jump	

1 **Work with a partner. Look at the words in the box. Choose a verb. Don't tell your partner. Draw a picture. Can your partner guess which verb it is?**

Adverbs of manner

badly	easily	quietly	quickly
carefully	happily	slowly	well

1 **Look at the words in the box for one minute. Close your books and write down the eight adverbs. Then open your books and check your spelling.**

2 **Work with a partner. Think of some things you do every day, e.g. *get up, have breakfast, walk to school,* etc. Then write sentences with these things and the adverbs.**

We have breakfast quickly and we walk to school slowly.

Explore expressions

1 **Complete the questions with a verb and the prepositions in the box. The same verb is missing in each one. What is it?**

up	through	after	like	out	for

1. Do you ever have to .... younger brothers, sisters or cousins? When?
2. How often do you .... your homework carefully before you give it to your teacher?
3. If you can't find your mobile phone, where do you .... it?
4. Who do you .... in your family?
5. When was the last time you shouted '.... .... !' at someone? What happened?
6. If you don't know the meaning of a word, do you .... it .... in a dictionary?

2 **Work with a partner. Ask and answer the questions in Exercise 1.**

Explore nouns with *-er*

build	farm	photograph	swim
explore	island	shop	paint

1 **Write nouns with *-er* using the words in the box above.**

2 **Add more nouns with *-er* to your list.**

3 **Draw a picture of one of your words. Your partner must guess the word. Then swap.**

Study tip

If it's difficult to think of a definition for the new words in your vocabulary notebook or on your cards, then draw a picture to help you remember the meaning.

Vocabulary Bank

Jog your memory!

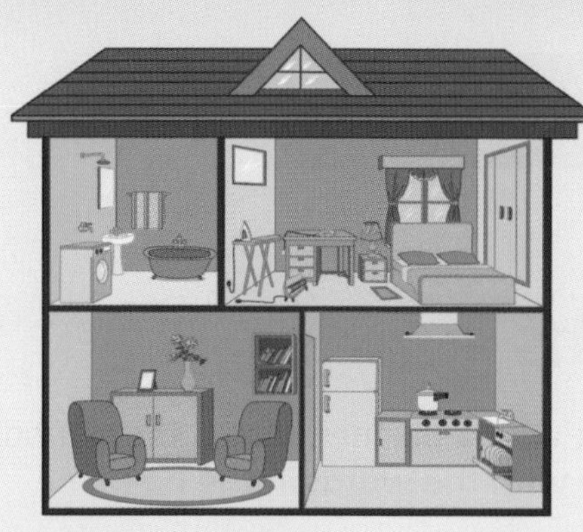

1 **Cover the rest of the page. How many things in the home and household appliances can you remember?**

Things in the home

blanket	cupboard	desk	mirror	towel
carpet	curtains	pillow	shelf	wardrobe

1 **Write the words from the box in the correct column. Some words can go in more than one column.**

bedroom	bathroom	living room	kitchen
blanket			

2 **Add two more new words to each column.**

Household appliances

cooker	fridge	iron
dishwasher	hairdryer	lamp
freezer	heater	washing machine

1 **Look at the words for one minute. Then close your book. Write down the household appliances. Open your book and check your spelling. How many are correct?**

2 **Write down the household appliances in order of the most useful to least useful.**

3 **Compare your list with a partner.**

Explore expressions with *do*

the washing	the ironing	sports	homework
housework	the washing	Maths	

1 **Look at the words in the box. Which of the things do you enjoy/not enjoy doing? Think of some more words to add to the list.**

2 **Write five sentences about you and the people you know. Use *do* and five of the words in the box.**

3 **Work with a partner. Don't show him/her your sentences. Read your sentence without the word(s) after *do*. Can your partner guess the word(s)?**

Explore verbs with *up* or *down*

go up / down	put up / down
get / come up	sit down / stand up

1 **Complete the sentences with the correct form of some of the verbs in the box.**

1 I usually .... in the morning when the sun .... .
2 We always .... when the teacher comes in the classroom. We can .... when she tells us.
3 I'm going to .... some pictures on my wall.
4 It takes a lot longer to .... the hill on a bicycle than it does to .... it.
5 .... your pens and listen.

2 **Work with a partner. Think of more verbs with *up* or *down*. (think of verbs of movement e.g. walk, climb, etc.). Write sentences with the verbs.**

Study tip

When you write down a word, make sure you spell it correctly. Then, when you learn the word, remember to learn the correct spelling too!

cupboard → p
silent

Maths Percentages

1 **Work with a partner. Match the symbols in the table with the words in the box.**

minus divide plus per cent
equals multiply (by) / times

symbol	+	−	×	÷	%	=
name	1 ...	2 ...	3 ...	4 ...	5 ...	6 ...

2 1.37 **Read and listen to the text. Which symbols from Exercise 1 do you use to calculate a percentage?**

3 **Read the text again and answer the questions.**

1 Where does the word 'per cent' come from?
2 Who first used the numbers 0-9?
3 Why do we use percentages?
4 What percentage is 'the whole' equal to?
5 What is the whole in the example with cakes?
6 What do we multiply the fraction by to get the final percentage?

Your turn

4 **Work with a partner. Calculate the percentage of chocolates that each person eats. Use the text to help you. The box has 60 chocolates.**

	Chocolates	Percentage of whole box
James	12	1 ....
Susan	6	2 ....
Ahmed	15	3 ....
Susie	20	4 ....

PERCENTAGES

The word 'per cent' comes from Roman times. It comes from the Latin words *per centum* or 'out of 100'. Before the Romans, the ancient Egyptians used a similar system of numbers in tens. But the numbers from 0 to 9 that we use today come from the ancient Arab world, over 2,000 years ago. The Arabs also used fractions, for example, ¼ . We use percentages to calculate how much a part of a whole is. And when we say 'per cent', we're really saying 'out of 100'.

50% OF THIS BOX IS BLUE (50 OUT OF 100)

25% OF THIS BOX IS (25 OUT OF 100)

When we calculate a percentage of something, first we need to know the total number of things, or 'the whole'. The whole is 100%. For example, there are 12 cakes on a table. In this calculation, 12 is the whole and is 100%.

Next, we need to know the number we want to change to a percentage. For example, Tanya eats three of the cakes on the table so three is the number we want to change to a percentage.

We put these two numbers into a fraction. In our example, we need to calculate what percent three (number of cakes Tanya ate) is of twelve (total number of cakes). The fraction is 3/12. 3 ÷ 12 = 0.25.

Finally, we multiply this number by 100 to make a percentage. 0.25 x 100 = 25.

So Tanya ate 25% of the cakes.

Find out about our number system.

History The feudal system

1 Match the words in the box with the pictures.

knight noble peasants king

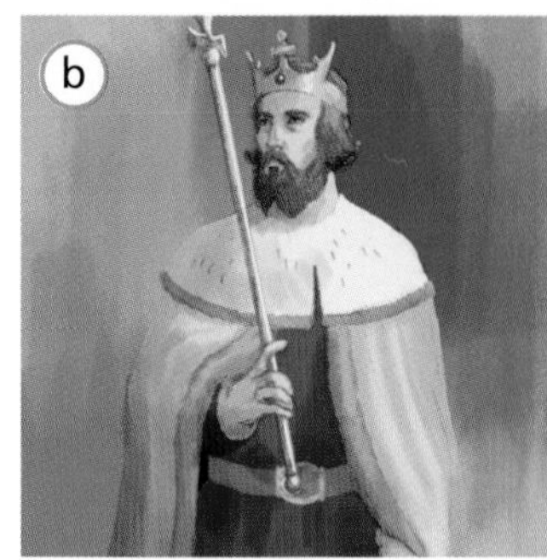

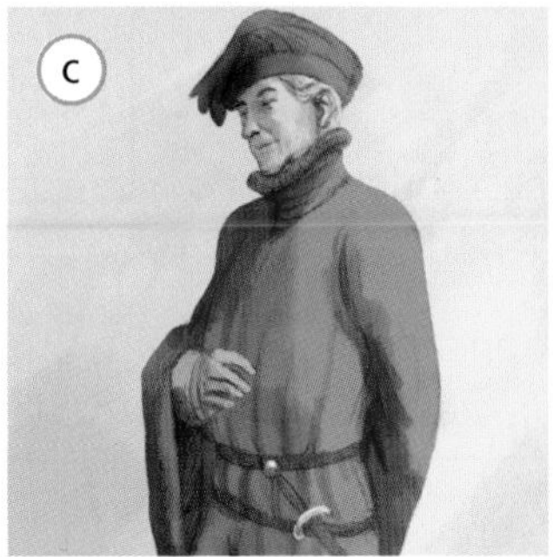

2 1.38 Read and listen to the text. Complete the article with the people in Exercise 1.

3 Choose the correct answers.

1 The king gave his land to nobles **to sell / to look after**.
2 When a king died, **his son / the noble** inherited the fief.
3 Nobles helped the king **in battles / find more land**.
4 Knights were **never / sometimes** women.
5 Peasants were **at the bottom / in the middle** of the feudal system.
6 Peasants paid taxes to **knights / nobles**.

Your turn

4 Work with a partner. Answer the questions.

1 What do you think of the feudal system? Was it fair? Why?/Why not?
2 Can you think of any famous knights from history?
3 Would you like to live in the Middle Ages? Why?/Why not?

THE FEUDAL SYSTEM

In Europe in the Middle Ages – from the 5th to the 15th century – some people owned land and some people lived or worked on the land. This system was called the feudal system. It was a hierarchy because some people were at the top and some people were at the bottom.

1 The [1]................... was at the top of the feudal system. He owned too much land to look after by himself so he divided it up, and gave some of it to people called 'nobles' to rule for him. These different areas of land were called fiefs. When a king died, his son became the owner of the fiefs.

2 The [2]................... looked after the king's land. They ruled large fiefs. They paid tax to the king and sometimes helped him in wars and battles. These people were less important than the king in the hierarchy but very important in the local community.

3 Nobles usually employed [3]................... to help protect their fiefs. They were often heroes because they were strong and brave, especially in battles. They always helped the king when he asked them and protected him. Most of them were men, but some were women.

4 About 90% of people in the Middle Ages were [4]................... . They were at the bottom of the hierarchy. They didn't have land or money like the other members of society. They worked on the land for the nobles, growing food and looking after animals. They paid taxes to the nobles and worked all day. Life was very hard for these people.

Find out about one of the first female pilots.

2.4 Amelia Earhart, famous flyer

Art Making a comic

1 Match the comic words with the definitions.

1 plot
2 panel
3 pencilling
4 a sketch
5 layout
6 inking
7 speech bubble
8 lettering

a the position of artwork on a page
b shape containing a character's words
c writing text in a speech bubble
d drawing something in pencil
e drawing something in pen
f a square or rectangular section of a comic
g the story of a comic
h a simple, basic drawing

2 1.39 Read and listen to the text and check your ideas to Exercise 1.

3 Read the text again. Mark the sentences true (*T*) or false (*F*). Correct the false sentences.

1 A comic usually begins with the artwork.
2 The writer sometimes draws parts of the comic.
3 The artist inks the artwork before pencilling it.
4 Computers usually do lettering.
5 The artist decides the position of speech bubbles.
6 The colourist colours the comic by hand.

Your turn

4 Work with a partner. Design your own comic. Follow the steps in the text.

The Art of Comics

Before an artist starts to draw, a comic generally begins with a 'plot'. The plot is the story of the comic. The comic writer sometimes plans the plot on the page and includes notes, basic sketches and instructions on what happens in each panel or section for the artist to interpret.

'Catman' carries the boy to safety. He puts him on the ground. Catman has a cat-like face, claws and is muscular with a superhero costume. Both boys look happy and very suprised.

When the writer finishes the plot, the artist pencils the story. This is when the artist does a sketch, or a simple basic drawing, of each panel in pencil. During pencilling, the artist decides the layout, position and style of the artwork. After this, the artist then 'inks' the sketches. In this process the artist creates clear, 'line art' in pen. It is still common for the artist to do the pencilling and inking by hand, not on computer.

Next, the artist inserts the dialogue into the speech bubbles. This is called 'lettering'. To do this, the artist usually uses a computer, but they must still plan by hand where the text goes on the page.

Finally, the artist adds colour to the final line art drawings. In the past, the artist did this by hand, but these days they use computers. The artist usually scans hand-drawn inked pages, and sends them to a colourist. The colourist then uses a special computer program to colour the images.

Find out about making a documentary.

Discovery EDUCATION

3.4 Behind the scenes

Art The Bauhaus movement

1 Look at the photos. Which words in the box can you use to describe each building?

modern old-fashioned practical
comfortable functional attractive simple

a

b

2 1.40 Read and listen to the text. Which building in Exercise 1 do you think is Bauhaus?

Bauhaus was an art school in Weimar, Germany. German architect Walter Gropius started the school in 1919. The Bauhaus school tried to combine form (the shape of something) and function (how we use something) in architecture so that buildings were practical but also simple. Bauhaus architects didn't like lots of decoration on buildings; they preferred flat roofs, straight lines and geometric shapes. Before Bauhaus, architects used lots of different shapes and colours, and materials like marble, hardwoods and even gold for the decorations in their buildings. Bauhaus used metal, glass, steel or plastic to make their buildings. Typical colours are white, grey and black. The designs for the furniture inside Bauhaus buildings are also simple, and functional.

3 Read the text again. Mark the sentences true *(T)* or false *(F)*. Correct the false sentences.

1 The Bauhaus style began in a school in Germany.
2 Bauhaus buildings are traditional and attractive.
3 The buildings used more basic materials than in the past.
4 You can only see the Bauhaus style in buildings and architecture.

4 1.41 Listen to the second part of the text about the Bauhaus school and choose the correct answers.

1 The Bauhaus school moved location twice / three times before it closed.
2 Former students of the school took their ideas to different parts of the world / Germany.
3 A building in an airport in Chicago / Houston is an example of Bauhaus architecture.
4 Josep Lluis Sert / Joan Miró designed the *Casa Bloc* in Barcelona.

Your turn

5 Work with a partner. Answer the questions.

1 Can you think of any buildings with a similar style to Bauhaus in your town or city?
2 Which buildings do you like in your town or city? What are they made of? What do you like about them?

Find out about the pyramids in Egypt.

Discovery EDUCATION
4.4 The seventh wonder of the world

Project 1

A sponsored event

SIXFIELDS ANIMAL HOSPITAL

Charity Day

at the Village Hall

Join the fun and help us reach our total of £5,000

Saturday 20th August

1 pm

Raffle

52155454

food and drink

Sponsored events:

fun run

dance marathon

Hot dog eating contest

music from local band, 'The Singrazers'

Look

1 Look at the poster about the charity day and answer the questions.

1 What is the charity?
2 Where is the charity day?
3 What day is it?
4 What time does it start?
5 What sponsored events are there?
6 What entertainment is there?
7 How much money do they want to raise?

Prepare

2 Work in groups of three. Plan a charity day in your town and make a poster. Use the questions in Exercise 1 to help you and find photos to put on your poster.

Present

3 Present your poster to the rest of the class. Give extra details about the charity, how friends and family can sponsor you, and the amount of money you want to raise. Which charity day is the class's favourite?

Project 2

A plan of my ideal house

Look

1 Look at the picture of an ideal house and complete the description with the words from the box.

wardrobe armchairs bathrooms fridge kitchen shelf

My house has got a lot of rooms. Upstairs there are two bedrooms, a games room and two [1]…. . Downstairs there's a living room, a big [2]…. , a swimming pool, a gym and a garden. My bedroom has got a massive [3]…. for all my clothes, mirrors on all of the walls, a king-sized bed, and two big chests of drawers. In the games room, there's a pool table, a big games centre, with games consoles and a big TV. There's also a [4]…. full of books, manga comics and computer games. Downstairs the living room is very comfortable with two sofas and four [5]…. , a coffee table and a cinema-sized TV on the wall. The kitchen's got two microwaves, three dishwashers and a big [6]…. and freezer for all my food.

Prepare

2 Work in groups of three. Imagine you live together. Design your ideal house and draw a simple plan of it. Think about …

- rooms and what you do in them.
- furniture and what you use it for.
- any other unusual or luxury items.

Present

3 Present your poster to the rest of the class. Which house is the class's favourite?

Thanks and acknowledgements

The authors and publishers would like to thank all the teachers and consultants who have contributed to the development of this course, in particular:

Argentina: Fernando Armesto; Natalia Bitar; Verónica Borrás; Leonor Corradi; Paz Moltrasio; Diana Ogando; Brazil: Dalmo Carvalho; Roberto Costa; Sônia M. B. Leites; Gloria Paz; Litany Pires Ribeiro; Christina Riego; Renata Condi de Souza; Elizabeth White; Chile: Magdalena Aldunate; M. Cristina Darraidou Diaz; Valentina Donoso; Ana María Páez Jofrré; Ricardo Contreras Marambio; Claudia Ottone; Maria Elena Ramirez; Jacqueline Rondon; Alicia Paez Ubilla; Colombia: Luz Amparo Bautista; Sonia Ruiz Hernández; Sandra Jara; Fabian Jimenez; Bibiana Andrea Piñeros Merizalde; Lucero Amparo Bernal Nieto; Olga Olarte; Bibiana Piñeros; Emelis Rambut; Sonia Ruíz; Poland: Anna Bylicka; Russia: Natalya Melchenkova; Irina Polyakova; Svetlana Suchkova; Irina Vayserberg; Turkey: Ali Bilgin; Angela Çakır; Shirley Nuttal; Cinla Sezgin; Mujgan Yesiloglu

The publishers are grateful to the following for permission to reproduce copyright photographs and material:

Cover: Shutterstock Images/Vibrant Image Studio; Back cover: Alamy/©Marc Hill; p. 7 (BL): Shutterstock Images/Zaretska Olga; p. 8 (B/G): Alamy/©imageimage; p. 9 (a): Alamy/©Peter Wheeler; p. 9 (b): Alamy/©Chloe Johnson; p. 9 (c): Alamy/©Travel Norwich - Chris Ridley; p. 9 (d): Alamy/©Robert Llewellyn; p. 9 (e): Alamy/©Janine Wiedel Photolibrary; p. 9 (f): Alamy/©Tom Merton; p. 9 (g): Alamy/©Gordon Scammell; p. 9 (h): Alamy/©Kumar Sriskandan; p. 9 (i): Alamy/©Iryna Vlasenko; p. 9 (j): Alamy/©David R. Frazier Photolibrary Inc.; p. 10 (TC): Alamy/©Peter Alvey People; p. 10 (a): Alamy/©Kumar Sriskandan; p. 10 (b): Alamy/©Caro; p. 10 (c): Alamy/©D. Hurst; p. 10-11 (d): Getty Images/Richard I'Anson/Lonely Planet Image; p. 12 (TL): Shutterstock Images/indigolotos; p. 12 (TC): Shutterstock Images/Everything; p. 12 (TR): Alamy/©momo_leif; p. 12 (CL): Shutterstock Images/Surrphoto; p. 12 (CR): Shutterstock Images/Feng Yu; p. 12 (BL): Shutterstock Images/anat chant; p. 12 (BR): Shutterstock Images/tale; p. 14 (B/G): Shutterstock Images/Enciktat; p. 14 (TL): Newscom/imago stock&people; p. 15 (CR): Alamy/©Chloe Parker; p. 15 (BC): Comic Relief/©Helen Hasse; p. 15 (BR): Alamy/©David Taylor; p. 16 (CR): Mark Bassett/Cambridge University Press; p. 16 (BL): Shutterstock Images/Chiyacat; p. 16 (BC): Shutterstock Images/sagir; p. 16 (BR): Thinkstock/Paolo_Toffanin/iStock; p. 17 (CL): Alamy/©John Fedele/Blend Images; p. 18 (B/G): Getty Images/Aurora Creative; p. 19 (a): Shutterstock Images/Mavkate; p. 19 (b): Alamy/©AberCPC; p. 19 (c): Shutterstock Images/Chutima Chaochaiya; p. 19 (d): Alamy/©Bill Stormont; p. 19 (e): Alamy/©Jack Sullivan; p. 19 (f): Alamy/©Hybrid Images/Cultura Creative (RF); p. 19 (g): Alamy/©RGB Ventures/SuperStock; p. 19 (h): Shutterstock Images/Diego Cervo; p. 19 (i): Alamy/©Jose Luis Pelaez/Blend Images; p. 19 (j): Alamy/©Steve Smith/Purestock; p. 20 (TL): Alamy/©Archive Images; p. 20 (TR): Alamy/©Rachel Megawhat; p. 21 (TL): Alamy/©Pictorial Press; p. 21 (CR): Alamy/©Photo Researchers; p. 24 (T): Corbis/Government of Chile/Handout; p. 25 (BR): Alamy/©ZUMA Press; p. 25 (C): Getty Images/Pascal Le Segretain; p. 25 (B/G): Alamy/©Ian Dagnall; p. 26 (TL): Alamy/©Liam White; p. 26 (TC): Thinkstock/Jupiterimages/Photos.com; p. 26 (CR): REX; p. 26 (BC): Getty Images /Joe Scarnici/USOC; p. 26 (BR): Alamy/©Keystone Pictures USA; p. 27 (TL): Alamy/©Geraint Lewis; p. 30 (B/G): Shutterstock Images/Jarno Gonzalez Zarraonandia; p. 32 (BR): Rex Feature/John Alex Maguire; p. 36 (TR): Alamy/©Chad Ehlers; p. 36 (B/G): Alamy/©Silvia Groniewicz; p. 37 (B): Shutterstock Images/Alberto Loyo; p. 38 (R): Alamy/©Ron Nickel/Design Pics Inc.; p. 40 (B/G): Thinkstock/flocu/iStock; p. 42 (a): Newscom/CB2/ZOB; p. 42 (b): Alamy/©Thierry GRUN; p. 42-43 (c): Alamy/©Jason Lindsey; p. 43 (CR): Alamy/©Ian Dagnall; p. 44 (TR): Alamy/©Ton Koene; p. 44 (C): Alamy/©brt CIRCUS; p. 44 (CR): Alamy/©Chuck Franklin; p. 44 (a): Alamy/©a-ts; p. 44 (b): Shutterstock Images/omers; p. 44 (c): Shutterstock Images/sue yassin; p. 44 (d): Shutterstock Images/Mile Atanasov; p. 44 (e): Alamy/©Leslie Garland/LGPL; p. 44 (f): Shutterstock Images/ppart; p. 44 (g): Alamy/©Andrii Gorulko; p. 44 (h): Shutterstock Images/Frank Mac; p. 44 (i): Shutterstock Images/ABB Photo; p. 45 (TR): Shutterstock Images/ChameleonsEye; p. 46 (CR): Alamy/©Don Fuchs; p. 46 (B/G): Alamy/©David Foster; p. 47 (B/G): Alamy/©Vicki Beaver; p. 47 (BC): Alamy/©Alaska Stock LLC; p. 48 (CR): Mark Bassett/Cambridge University Press; p. 50 (a): Shutterstock Images/Bonchan; p. 50 (b): Shutterstock Images/VadiCo; p. 50 (c): Shutterstock Images/Elnur; p. 50 (d): Shutterstock Images/Margouillat photo; p. 50 (e): Shutterstock Images/Africa Studio; p. 53 (a): Shutterstock Images/gillmar; p. 53 (b): Shutterstock Images/Alexey Boldin; p. 53 (c): Shutterstock Images/GeorgeMPhotography; p. 53 (d): Shutterstock Images/Sean Nel; p. 53 (e): Shutterstock Images/AG-PHOTO; p. 53 (f): Shutterstock Images/Maksym Dykha; p. 53 (g): Shutterstock Images/Dmitry Melnikov; p. 53 (h): Shutterstock Images/Sergey Peterman; p. 53 (i): Shutterstock Images/RMIKKA; p. 54 (B/G, CR): REX/Bruce Adams; p. 54 (TL): Shutterstock Images/sgm; p. 55 (BL): Alamy/©Pictorial Press; p. 56 (TR): REX/Gavin Roberts/Future Publishing; p. 59 (b): Alamy/©Jochen Schlenker/Robert Harding Picture Library Ltd; p. 59 (TR): Getty Images/Hero Images/Digital Vision; p. 60 (TR): Glow Images/Tetra Images; p. 62 (B/G): Getty Images/Uppercut/Spike Mafford; p. 63 (a): Glow Images/AID/a.collectionRF; p. 63 (b): Alamy/©Terry Vine/Blend Images; p. 63 (c): Alamy/©Angela Hampton/Bubbles Photolibrary; p. 63 (d): Alamy/©Robert Kerr; p. 63 (e): Alamy/©James Brunker; p. 63 (f): Alamy/©philipus; p. 63 (g): Alamy/©aberystwyth; p. 63 (h): Alamy/©Zoonar GmbH/Darya Petrenko; p. 63 (i): Alamy/©Kentaroo Tryman; p. 63 (j): Alamy/©MBI; p. 66 (TR): Superstock/Photononstop; p. 66 (a): Getty Images/Jamie Grill/Photodisc; p. 66 (b): Shutterstock Images/jocic; p. 66 (c): Thinkstock/Michael Dykstra/Hemera; p. 66 (d): Shutterstock Images/Roman Samokhin; p. 66 (e): Shutterstock Images/R. Gino Santa Maria; p. 66 (f): Shutterstock Images/MNI; p. 66 (g): Shutterstock Images/maxim ibragimov; p. 66 (h): Alamy/©Studiomode; p. 67 (BL): Alamy/©Jeff Morgan 04; p. 68 (CL): Shutterstock Images/canadastock; p. 68 (B/G): Alamy/©Anna Omelchenko; p. 68 (C): Shutterstock Images/Hugh Lansdown; p. 69 (T): Alamy/©Linda Schaefer; p. 69 (B): Alamy/©Susan Liebold; p. 69 (C): Alamy/©szefei wong; p. 70 (CL): Agefotostock/Jeff Greenberg; p. 71 (TR): Mark Bassett/Cambridge University Press; p. 72 (CL): Getty Images/Hero Images/Digital Vision; p. 74 (B/G): Alamy/©artpartner.de; p. 76 (TR): Media Ltd/©ncj; p. 76 (BC): Shutterstock Images/Nattika; p. 76 (BL): Shutterstock Images/Krivosheev Vitaly; p. 76 (CR): Shutterstock Images/STILLFX; p. 76 (CL): Shutterstock Images/Dim Dimich; p. 76 (TC): Shutterstock Images/Susan Schmitz; p. 76 (TL): Shutterstock Images/panbazil; p. 77 (C): REX/Isifa Image Service sro; p. 78 (B): Shutterstock Images/jur_ziv; p. 78 (TL): iStock/teekid; p. 78 (TR): Alamy/©Paul Maguire; p. 79 (CR): Alamy/©Flashgun/Cultura Creative (RF); p. 80 (TL): Shutterstock Images/Brberrys; p. 80 (CL): Photo Researchers/FLPA; p. 80 (B/G): Alamy/©RIA Novosti; p. 80 (CR): Alamy/©Robert Pickett/Papilio; p. 81 (B): Shutterstock Images/Matt Gibson; p. 82 (CR): Alamy/©Chris Rout; p. 82 (BR): Alamy/©Monty Rakusen/Cultura Creative; p. 82 (CL): Getty images/kali9; p. 83 (TR): Thinkstock/BananaStock; p. 84 (B/G): Alamy/©David Wall; p. 85 (a): Alamy/©Matelly/Cultura RM; p. 85 (b): Alamy/©Odilon Dimier/PhotoAlto; p. 85 (c): Alamy/©Denise Hager/Catchlight Visual Services; p. 85 (d): Alamy/©Sally and Richard Greenhill; p. 85 (e): Alamy/©Image Source; p. 85 (f): Alamy/©Tim Hall/Cultura Creative; p. 85 (g): Alamy/©Tim Hall/Cultura Creative; p. 85 (h): Alamy/©Mai Chen; p. 85 (i): Alamy/©keith morris; p. 85 (j): Alamy/©Mikhail Lavrenov; p. 86 (TC): AgeFotostock/YURI ARCURS; p. 86 (TR): Alamy/©HermesMereghetti; p. 86 (BL): Alamy/©TravelStockCollection - Homer Sykes; p. 88 (TR): Alamy/©ZUMA Press Inc; p. 88 (TC): Alamy/©LHB Photo; p. 88 (TL): Alamy/©Bill Bachman; p. 90 (CR): Shutterstock Images/foodfoto; p. 90 (T): Shutterstock Images/Romiana Lee; p. 92 (C): Alamy/©David Grossman; p. 92 (CR): Getty Images/MCT; p. 92 (BC): REX/Andrew Price; p. 92 (BR): Alamy/©Manfred Grebler; p. 93 (TR): Alamy/©Moxie Productions/Blend Images; p. 109 (TR): Alamy/©Blend Images; p. 109 (TC): Alamy/©Bill Stormont; p. 113 (TR): Alamy/©MBI; p. 113 (TC): Thinkstock/Michael Dykstra/Hemera; p. 115 (TR): Alamy/©Cultura Creative (RF); Alamy/©Bill Stormont; p. 119 (a): Shutterstock Images/Claudio Divizia; p. 119 (b): Alamy/©AlanWrigley; p. 119 (CL): REX/Tony Kyriacou; p. 120 (TR): Alamy/©Everett Collection Historical; p. 121 (TL): Thinkstock/Zoonar RF; p. 121 (TCL): Shutterstock Images/Barbro Bergfeldt; p. 121 (TCR): Alamy/ ©Spectral; p. 121 (TR): Thinkstock/TongRo Images; p. 121 (B): Thinkstock/defun/iStock; p. 122 (CR): Alamy/©Pete Titmuss; p. 122 (CL): Shutterstock Images/ Viktor1; p. 122 (C): Alamy/©Cultura RM; p. 123 (1): Shutterstock Images/Ivan Pavlov; p. 123 (2): Alamy/©eye35.pix; p. 123 (3): Alamy/©Topsy; p. 126 (TL): Alamy/©International Photobank; p. 126 (TR): Alamy/©Jack Sullivan; p. 126 (CR): Alamy/©Paul Gapper.

The publishers are grateful to the following illustrators:

Janet Allinger p. 13, 56, 61, 112; David Belmonte (Beehive Illustration): p. 12, 75, 78, 94, 114; Anni Betts p. 6, 34 (T), 58 (C), 87 (R), 116; Galia Bernstein (NB Illustration): p. 32, 88, 108, 115; Seb Camagajevac p. 117; Russ Cook p. 28 (B), 34 (B), 110 (TR); A Corazon p. 116; Nigel Dobbyn (Beehive Illustration): p. 4, 31, 39, 56, 57, 91 (BR), 110 (TC), 112, 118; Mark Duffin p. 28 (T), 41, 60, 125; emc p. 5; Bob Lea p. 52; Q2A Media Services, Inc. p. 10, 14, 15, 22, 24, 25, 36, 37, 46, 47, 49, 58 (TR), 59, 64, 68, 69, 80, 81, 87 (L), 90, 91 (CR), 111; Sean Tiffany p. 22, 49, 64, 87 (L).

All video stills by kind permission of:

Discovery Communications, LLC 2015: p. 8 (1, 2, 4), 11, 14, 18 (1, 2, 4), 21, 24, 30 (1, 2, 4), 33, 36, 40 (1, 2, 4), 43, 46, 52 (1, 2, 4), 55, 58, 62 (1, 2, 4), 65, 68, 74 (1, 2, 4), 77, 80, 84 (1, 2, 4), 87, 90, 116, 117, 118, 119, 190, 121, 122, 123;

Cambridge University Press: p. 8 (3), 16, 18 (3), 26, 30 (3), 38, 40 (3), 48, 52 (3), 60, 62 (3), 70, 74 (3), 82, 82 (3), 92.

The publishers are grateful to the following contributors:

Blooberry and emc design limited: concept design
emc design limited: text design and layouts
QBS Learning: cover design and photo selection
Ian Harker and dsound: audio recordings
Integra Software Services Pvt. Ltd.: video production
Nick Bruckman and People's TV: voxpop video production
Hart McCleod: video voiceovers
Anna Whitcher: video management
Jeremy Bowell: editorial services
Getty Images: music

Vicki Anderson with **Eoin Higgins**

Contents

Starter Unit

Family

1 ★ Put the letters in order to make family words.

1 umm *mum*
2 dda ______
3 madrang ______
4 enrpast ______
5 leunc ______
6 rtborhe ______
7 fewi ______
8 trisse ______
9 natu ______
10 sicuno ______
11 dradngad ______
12 baunsdh ______

2 ★★ Match the words in Exercise 1 to make pairs.

1 wife – *husband*
2 uncle – ______
3 grandma – ______
4 dad – ______
5 brother – ______

3 ★★★ Complete the definitions.

1 My mum and dad are my *parents* .
2 My aunt's husband is my ______ .
3 My granddad's wife is my ______ .
4 My aunt's children are my ______ .
5 My grandma and granddad are my ______ .
6 My dad's wife is my ______ .
7 My mum and dad's child is my ______ or ______ .

Subject pronouns and *be*

4 ★ Circle the correct options.

1 Where am **I** / **you**?
2 **Is** / **Are** you from Canada?
3 Daniel **am** / **is** my cousin. **He** / **They** is 14.
4 My sister's birthday **are** / **is** in May.
5 My grandparents **are** / **is** in Japan. **She's** / **They're** on holiday.
6 My brother and I **am** / **are** at the zoo. **We** / **They** are not at school.
7 I **am** / **is** at the cinema. Are **you** / **he** at the shops?

be

5 ★★ Complete the sentences and questions with the correct form of *be*.

1 *Are* you at home?
2 This ______ my mum.
3 We ______ best friends.
4 ______ they from England?
5 His sister ______ in my class.
6 I ______ from Edinburgh, Scotland.
7 ______ you in the school football team?
8 My new dog ______ called Bob.

Possessive *'s*

6 ★ Complete the sentences with *'s* in the correct place.

1 My mum *'s* car is red.
2 Our cousin house is in the city.
3 Is this your granddad piano?
4 What's your dad name?
5 My best friend birthday is in October.
6 His sister dance classes are on Monday.
7 Is our dog nose brown?
8 Where is my brother T-shirt?

Starter Unit

School subjects

1 ★★ **Look at the pictures and complete the crossword with the school subjects.**

down

across

2 ★★ **Match the school subjects with the sentences.**

ICT Geography French ~~History~~
Maths PE Science English Music

1 'Let's talk about the year 1914.' *History*
2 'What does *je m'appelle* mean?' ________
3 'OK, run around the gym ten times.' ________
4 'Turn on the computers, please.' ________
5 'Let's play it again and listen to the piano.' ________
6 'Water is hydrogen and … what?' ________
7 'What is 15 x 147?' ________
8 'Where are the Rocky Mountains?' ________
9 'Let's look at the verb *to be*.' ________

there is/are and *some* and *any*

3 ★★ **Find five more differences between Picture A and Picture B and write sentences. Use *there is*(*n't*) / *there are*(*n't*).**

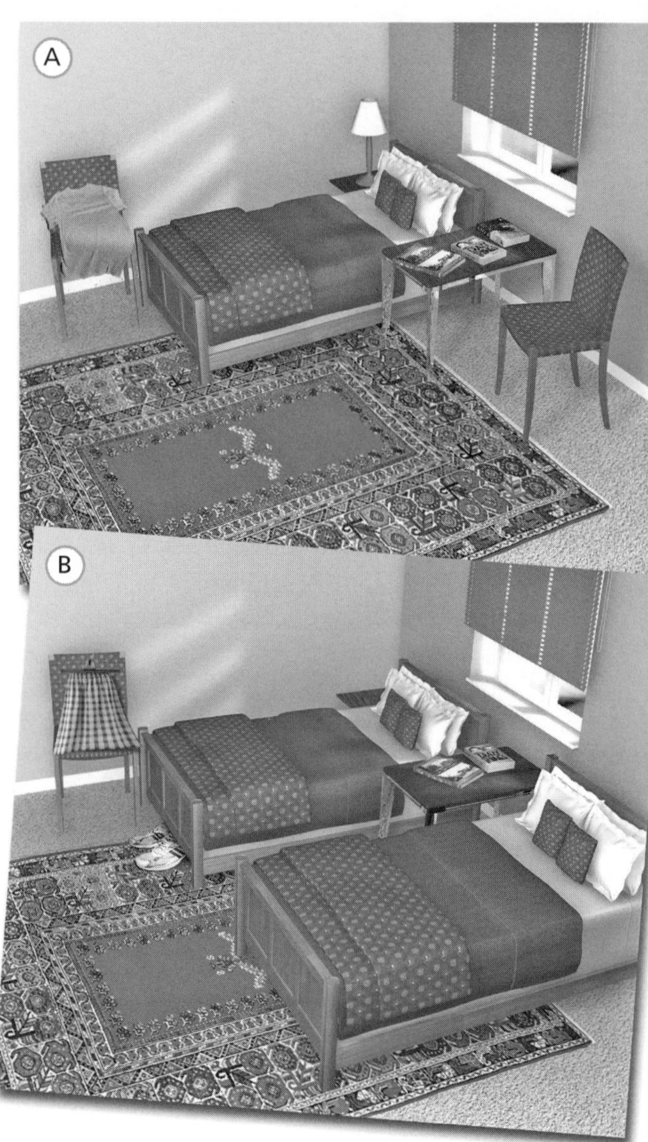

1 *In Picture A there are three books. In Picture B there are two.*
2 ________
3 ________
4 ________
5 ________
6 ________

Starter Unit

1 ★★ Circle the correct options and complete the sentences with *some* or *any*.

1 There **isn't / aren't** ___any___ cheese in the fridge.
2 **Are / Is** there __________ giraffes in the zoo?
3 **Is there / Are there** __________ T-shirts in your bag?
4 There **is / are** __________ fruit in the kitchen.
5 There **isn't / aren't** __________ boats on the river.
6 **Is there / Are there** __________ pasta in the cupboard?
7 There **is / are** __________ good photos on your mobile phone.
8 There **isn't / aren't** __________ money in my bag.

have got

2 ★ Circle the correct options.

1 I **'ve / 's** got a new computer.
2 **Have / Has** you got a mobile phone?
3 My sister **have / has** got a TV in her room.
4 We **'ve / 's** got a pet cat. His name is Peru.
5 **Have / Has** he got your phone number?
6 They **'ve / 's** got two houses in the city.
7 She **haven't / hasn't** got a brother.
8 Our dog **'ve / 's** got a tennis ball.
9 We **haven't / hasn't** got a big family.

Sports and activities

3 ★★ Put the letters in order to make sports and activities. Then complete the sentences with the correct form of *play*, *do* or *go*.

1 Do you ___play___ ___basketball___ at your school? (sblaltabke)
2 I'd like to __________ __________ in the evenings. (gyoa)
3 We __________ __________ in the mountains every winter. (gisnki)
4 Can you __________ __________? (yalolblelv)
5 My brother __________ __________ every Saturday. (duoj)
6 A lot of people __________ __________ in the sea in Ireland. (fnruisg)
7 My family sometimes __________ __________ in the lake. (mgnswmii)
8 Let's __________ __________ at the skate park later. (aasgbtdkineor)
9 Do you often __________ __________ with your friends? (libogwn)
10 I want to __________ __________ but my brother's got my bike. (liccgyn)

Present simple: affirmative and negative

4 ★ Circle the correct words in the grammar table.

1	I/You/We/They **watch / watches** TV.
2	He/She/It **finish / finishes** at five.
3	We **don't / doesn't** like carrots.
4	She **don't / doesn't** like bananas.

5 ★★ Complete the text with the present simple form of the verbs in brackets.

My family [1] ___loves___ (love) sport. We all [2] __________ (play) one sport or more. My dad [3] __________ (play) tennis every Saturday. My mum [4] __________ (go) to the gym and [5] __________ (do) yoga twice a week. I [6] __________ (do) karate after school and every weekend I [7] __________ (go) skateboarding with friends. My brother [8] __________ (play) basketball and he [9] __________ (train) four days a week. We often [10] __________ (go) to see him play. We [11] __________ (not watch) sport on TV because we [12] __________ (not like) watching TV.

Starter Unit

Present simple: *Yes/No* questions

1 ★ **Circle the correct words in the grammar table.**

1	**Do you / You** like karate?
2	Yes, I **do / does**. No, I **don't / doesn't**.
3	**He / Does he** play tennis?
4	Yes, he **do / does**. No, he **don't / doesn't**.

2 ★★ **Complete the questions and answers with the correct form of *do*.**

1 ___*Do*___ you do your homework in the evening? Yes, I ___*do*___ .
2 ________ Harry and Gina go cycling on Saturdays? No, they ________ .
3 ________ Nina like Geography? No, she ________ .
4 ________ your friends go skateboarding? Yes, they ________ .
5 ________ they use the Internet to study French? No, they ________ .
6 ________ your brother do karate? Yes, he ________ .
7 ________ your teacher show videos in English class? No, she ________ .

Present simple: *Wh-* questions

3 ★★ **Match the question words with the words in the box.**

person object/thing place ~~frequency~~ time reason

1 how often ___*frequency*___
2 what ________
3 when ________
4 where ________
5 who ________
6 why ________

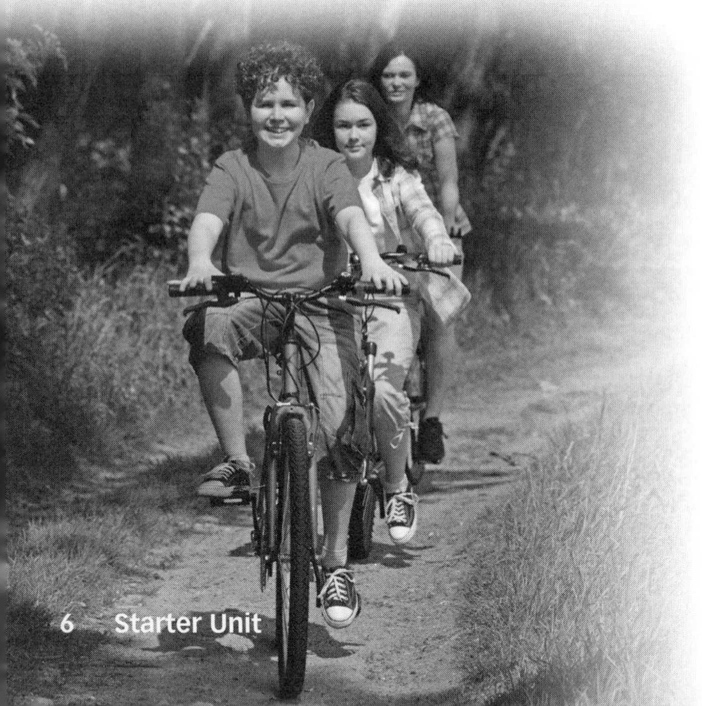

4 ★★ **Complete the questions with the correct question word from the box.**

How often What When ~~Where~~ Who Why Where

1 **A:** ___*Where do you live?*___ (you / live)
B: In London.
2 **A:** ________ does he study?
B: English and Maths.
3 **A:** ________ do they play sports?
B: Once a week.
4 **A:** ________ does he go cycling with?
B: His brother.
5 **A:** ________ do you like skateboarding?
B: Because it's fun.
6 **A:** ________ does she play volleyball?
B: In the park.
7 **A:** ________ does he go to drama class?
B: On Saturdays.

Adverbs of frequency

5 ★ **Circle the correct words in the grammar table.**

1	Going swimming with my friends **is always / always is** good fun.
2	We **go sometimes / sometimes go** to the sports centre on Saturdays.

6 ★★ **Put the words in the correct order to make sentences.**

1 football / play / school / at / We / always
We always play football at school.
2 Football / sometimes / matches / long / are / very
____
3 never / me / with / My dad / chess / plays
____
4 We / often / Saturdays / on / go / cycling
____
5 dictionaries / use / English class / usually / We / in
____
6 are / His / really interesting / books / always
____

1 Money matters

Vocabulary

Shops

1 ★ Find ten shops in the word search.

e	l	s	p	o	r	t	s	o	c	d
l	c	v	e	n	m	o	s	o	h	e
e	p	r	d	z	u	s	h	y	e	p
c	b	m	t	h	s	x	o	o	m	a
t	g	l	d	e	i	n	e	u	i	r
r	q	j	b	d	c	t	e	r	s	t
o	b	o	o	k	s	h	o	p	t	m
n	p	l	c	e	u	w	z	m	e	e
i	v	c	l	o	t	h	e	s	t	n
c	n	e	i	l	r	m	e	r	p	t
s	u	p	e	r	m	a	r	k	e	t
s	n	e	w	s	a	g	e	n	t	b

2 ★ Complete the table with the words from Exercise 1.

1 Five words that go with *shop*	
sports shop	___________ shop
___________ shop	___________ shop
___________ shop	
2 One word that goes with *store*	
___________ store	
3 Four words that are <u>ONE</u> word	
___________	___________
___________	___________

3 ★★ Complete the sentences with words from Exercise 1.

1. You can buy trainers and boots in a *shoe shop* .
2. I need some aspirin from the ___________ .
3. My favourite shop is the ___________ because it sells magazines and chocolate.
4. I like that ___________ because it's got great T-shirts and cheap jeans.
5. I'd like to look at some laptops – let's go to the ___________ .
6. Why don't you go to the ___________ to buy a book for your dad's birthday?
7. We're going to the ___________ to buy fruit, vegetables and some other things.
8. I like the guitars in this ___________ .

4 ★★ Complete the text with words from Exercise 1.

There is a shopping centre in my town, but my friends and I don't often go there. It's got a [1] *newsagent* where you can buy magazines or birthday cards, and a couple of [2]___________ with jeans and T-shirts, but nothing cool for teenagers. My mum and dad love the [3]___________ because you can find everything you need there. There are some shops I like. There's a [4]___________ with great trainers, and there's also an [5]___________ with lots of tablets and smartphones, but they're a bit expensive. My favourite is the [6]___________ because it plays all the new songs, and a lot of young people go there.

5 ★★★ Write about a shopping centre you know. Complete the sentences about it.

1. It's got a *big department store* .
2. There's a ___________ where you can buy ___________ and ___________ .
3. I like the ___________ because it's got ___________ .
4. I don't go to the ___________ because it hasn't got ___________ .
5. My mum and dad like the ___________ because ___________ .

Language focus 1

Present continuous

1 ★ **Circle the correct words in the grammar table.**

1	She **'s looking / looking** at boots in the shoe shop.
2	They **not buying / aren't buying** those T-shirts.
3	**Are you coming / You are coming** with us?
4	Yes, **I'm / I am**. No, we **aren't / isn't**.
5	To talk about facts, habits and routines, use the present **simple / continuous**.
6	To talk about an action in progress, use the present **simple / continuous**.

2 ★★ **Complete the conversations with the present continuous form of the verbs in brackets.**

Joe: Hi Bob. We're [1] *meeting* (meet) outside the shopping centre. Where are you?
Bob: I [2] ___________ (sit) on the bus. Where are you?
Joe: Outside the shopping centre. Ian and I [3] ___________ (wait) for you now.
Bob: OK. There's a lot of traffic. The bus [4] ___________ (not go) very fast.
Joe: Well, we [5] ___________ (not stay) here a long time. It's cold! Where's the bus now?
Bob: It [6] ___________ (come) into Mill Street, so see you in two minutes.

3 ★★ **Complete the questions and short answers with the correct form of the present continuous. Use the words in the box.**

you sell   we have   ~~he look~~
you spend   they buy   Lisa wait

1 *Is he looking for a book in English?*
Yes, he is.
2 ____________________ your old video games?
Yes, ___________ , for €5 each.
3 ____________________ that CD?
No, ___________ .
4 ____________________ lunch now?
No, ___________ , just a drink.
5 ____________________ in the café?
No, ___________ . She's late.
6 ____________________ £20 on a T-shirt?
Yes, ___________ . It's a present.

Present simple vs. continuous

4 ★★ **Circle the correct words in the text.**

My sister and I [1]**try / are trying** an experiment at the moment – no shopping for a month! Usually Mum [2]**gives / is giving** me pocket money on Saturday and my friends and I [3]**go / are going** shopping in the afternoon, but this Saturday is different. My friends [4]**shop / are shopping** for clothes and things but I [5]**write / 'm writing** this blog at home. Why? Well, I [6]**have / am having** a lot of things that I never [7]**wear / am wearing**. This month my sister Jane and I [8]**put / are putting** our pocket money in our money boxes for our holidays, and we [9]**do / are doing** lots of other things. Shopping all the time is boring!

5 ★★★ **Write the questions in the present simple or present continuous and answer them for you.**

1 What / wear / at the moment?
What are you wearing at the moment?
I'm wearing …
2 you / reading / a good book / at the moment?
____
____
3 Where / usually / buy your clothes?
____
____
4 you / listen to music? What / you / listen to?
____
____

Explore extreme adjectives

6 ★★ **Complete the definitions with the adjectives in the box.**

huge   ~~great~~   wonderful   amazing
brilliant   boiling   awful   freezing

1 When something is very good we say it's *great* , ___________ , ___________ or ___________ .
2 When it's very hot, we say it's ___________ .
3 When something is very big, we say it's ___________ .
4 When it's very cold, we say it's ___________ .
5 When something is very bad, we say it's ___________ .

Listening and vocabulary

Money verbs

1 ★ Match the verbs in the box with the correct definition.

sell spend save ~~earn~~ buy borrow

1 get money from working *earn*
2 get money from someone to keep for a short time ______
3 what a shop does ______
4 pay money to get something specific ______
5 use money for something, not only in shops ______
6 keep money so you can use it in the future ______

2 ★★ Complete the sentences with the verbs from Exercise 1.

1 I'm trying to *save* my pocket money for a new smartphone.
2 Jane wants to ______ all her video games for €10 each.
3 Can I ______ €5 from you until tomorrow?
4 Some people ______ a lot of money on clothes.
5 How much money does a shop assistant ______ ?
6 I want to ______ some new skates this year.

3 ★★★ Write the answers to the questions. Use the present continuous and the words in brackets.

1 What are you doing on ebay? (sell / my computer)
I'm selling my computer.
2 Why are you putting money in that box? (save for / new bike)
______
3 Why are you going to Helen's house? (borrow / her dress)
______
4 Why are you in the sports shop? (buy / new trainers)
______
5 What are you doing? (spend / five pounds / sweets!)
______
6 Why are you cleaning your dad's car? (earn / money / a new phone)
______

Listening

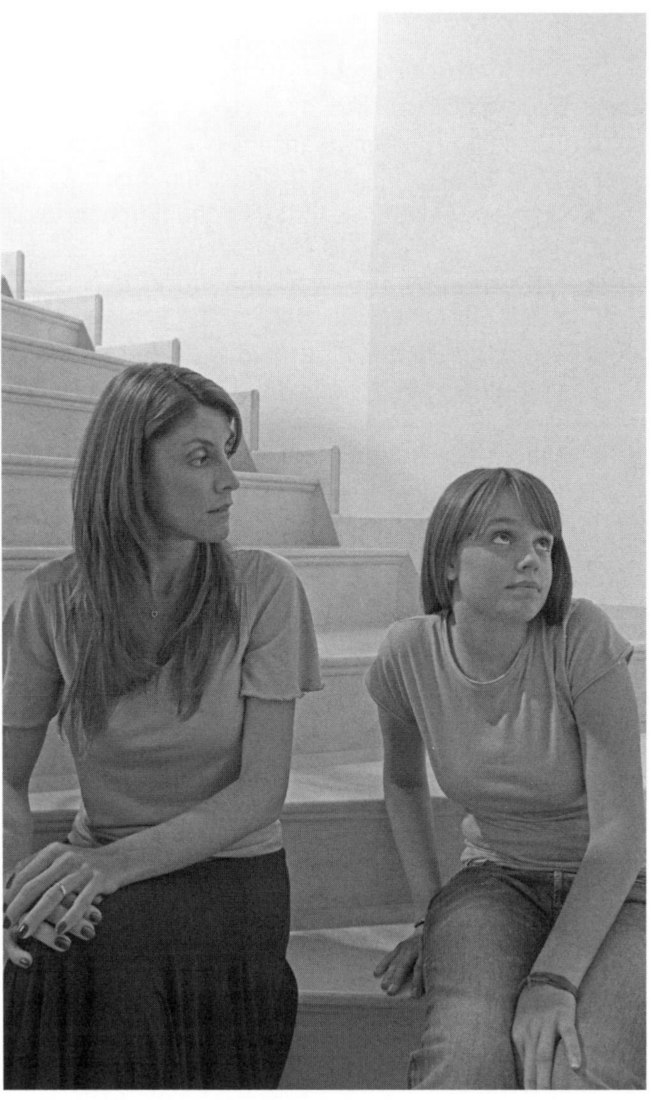

4 ★ 01 Listen to the conversation between Gemma and her mum. What is Gemma's problem? Circle the correct option.

a clothes b money c her brother

5 ★★ 01 Read the sentences. Listen again and circle the correct options.

1 Gemma wants to buy a pair of jeans **online** / **at the shopping centre**.
2 Gemma's pocket money is **£50** / **£30** a month.
3 **Gemma** / **Gemma's brother** saves money.
4 Gemma says she needs more money than her brother because **she's older** / **he only buys video games**.
5 The cinema costs **£5** / **£10**.
6 Her mum tells Gemma to **do work in their house** / **get a babysitting job**.
7 Gemma **likes** / **doesn't like** her mum's idea.
8 Gemma's mum gives her **more money** / **a job**.

Language focus 2

(*don't*) *want to, would*(*n't*) *like to, would prefer to*

1 ★ **Circle the correct options.**

1 **Would** / **Do** you like to save more money?
2 Would you **prefer / want** the black T-shirt or the white one?
3 I'd **want / like** to go to the electronics shop to see some new mobile phones.
4 She **doesn't want / wouldn't prefer** to borrow money from her sister.
5 Would you **like / want** to go to the bookshop?
6 I **wouldn't like / don't prefer** to buy a new car.

2 ★ **Match the questions with the answers.**

1 Does your friend want to come with us? *c*
2 Would you like to listen to music? ___
3 Would Barry prefer to go to the sports shop? ___
4 Do they want to invite Paul to come shopping? ___
5 Would Mary and Arthur like to go to a café? ___
6 Would Claudia prefer to do the exam today? ___

a Yes, he would.
b No, they wouldn't.
c No, she doesn't.
d Yes, she would.
e Yes, I would.
f Yes, they do.

3 ★★ **Complete the sentences with the correct form of the verbs in the box.**

sell spend play ~~go~~ earn buy

1 I don't want *to go* to a bookshop.
2 We'd really like ___________ more money.
3 I wouldn't like ___________ a lot of money on a phone.
4 Yolanda would prefer not ___________ some new trainers.
5 They want ___________ video games.

4 ★★★ **Complete the sentences with your own ideas.**

1 I'd prefer to eat …
___________ .
2 I wouldn't like to be …
___________ .
3 I don't want to go …
___________ .
4 I really want to be …
___________ .
5 In the future I would …
___________ .

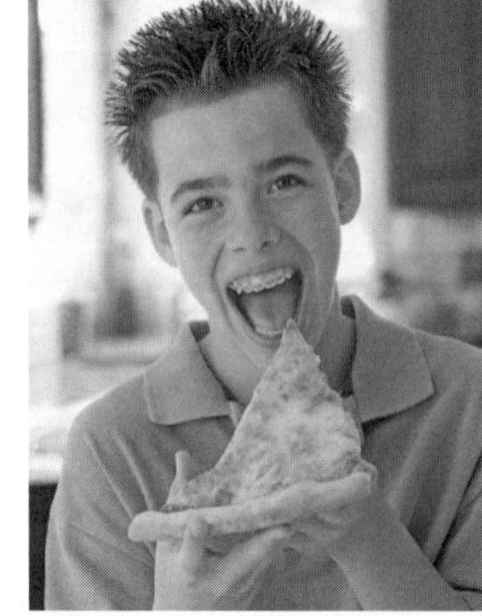

(*not*) *enough* + noun

5 ★★ **Match the sentence beginnings (1–6) with the sentence endings (a–f).**

1 We can't make a cake because … *e*
2 They're not dancing here because … ___
3 I can't do all my homework because … ___
4 A lot of people were still hungry because … ___
5 We can't all study for the exam because … ___
6 We want to buy a new tablet but … ___

a … there wasn't enough food.
b … we haven't got enough money.
c … there isn't enough space.
d … I haven't got enough time.
e … there aren't enough eggs.
f … there aren't enough books.

6 ★★★ **Read the problems and write a sentence with (*not*) *enough*.**

1 There are five T-shirts in the shop and 20 people want to buy one.
There aren't enough T-shirts in the shop.
2 I've got £20 and these jeans cost £15.
____
3 There are a lot of children in this town and there's only one small park.
____
4 We've got 10 bottles of water for 100 people.
____
5 She's got 30 minutes before her class to do this exercise.
____
6 We're going to make sandwiches for 30 people but we've only got 25 slices of bread.
____

Explore adjective prefixes

7 ★★ **Add the prefix *un-* to the adjectives and match them with the definitions.**

friendly ~~happy~~ usual tidy fair helpful

1 sad *unhappy*
2 different or not common ___________
3 not nice to another person ___________
4 not wanting to help someone ___________
5 when the rules are not the same for everyone ___________
6 when things are not clean or not in the right place ___________

Reading

1 ★ **Read the text about a new supermarket. What is different about it?**

SHOPPING BY PHONE

On the walls of an underground station in central Seoul, South Korea, there are a lot of pictures of food and drinks: bananas, meat, rice, coffee, even pet food. But these are not **advertisements**. This is the world's first 'virtual' supermarket, called *Homeplus*.

The supermarket is unusual because you use the special *Homeplus* app on your smartphone to go shopping. When you want to buy something, you use this **app** to scan the barcodes of the products you want. You put them in your online **shopping trolley** and then you pay by phone. You haven't got any heavy bags to carry because the supermarket **delivers** everything to your house for you.

South Koreans like shopping online and millions of them have smartphones, but are they ready for this type of shopping? 'Young Koreans use their smartphones to do a lot of different **tasks** every day,' says a *Homeplus* virtual store manager. 'Our customers work really hard and don't have enough time to go to the supermarket. Our store helps them save time.' So, is this the future?

2 ★★ **Complete the definitions with the words in bold from the text.**

1. ___*Tasks*___ are little jobs we do every day at work or at home.
2. Sometimes in the middle of a TV programme, they show ____________ .
3. An ____________ is a small computer program on your phone or tablet.
4. When you call a pizza company, it normally ____________ the pizzas to your house.
5. A ____________ is something you put your food in at the supermarket.

3 ★★ **Read the text again. Answer the questions.**

1. Where is the supermarket?
   It's in an underground station in Seoul.
2. What can you buy at the supermarket?
   ____
3. What do you need to buy things here?
   ____
4. What happens after you pay for your shopping?
   ____
5. Why does the store manager think it's good for Koreans?
   ____

4 ★★★ **Complete the advertisement for *Homeplus* with words from the text.**

HOMEPLUS
– the virtual supermarket

We help you save time!

1. Choose the f*ood*________ or d*rink*________ you want.
2. Scan the b__________ .
3. Fill your s__________ t__________ with food.
4. P__________ for your shopping with your p__________ .
5. *Homeplus* d__________ everything to your house.

5 ★★★ **What's good about a virtual shop like this? What's bad about it? Write at least five sentences.**

____
____
____
____
____

Writing

An email

1 **Read Jenny's email. What is her problem with money?**

Hi Gina,
I get £5 a week pocket money, but I spend it all. How can I save my money?
Please help!
Jenny

Hi Jenny,
I have the same problem! Try writing down everything you buy for a week and how much it costs. Do you spend a lot on food and drink, for example? Don't spend money on things you don't need. Make a sandwich at home, and don't buy sweets every day.
Put some money in your money box when you get it. Ask for five £1 coins so you can do this. Sometimes I try to earn some money from my family. Maybe you can do jobs, for example, wash the car or water the plants. But be realistic – £5 isn't a lot!
Good luck,
Gina

2 **Complete the table with Gina's advice.**

Do	Don't
write down everything you buy for a week	

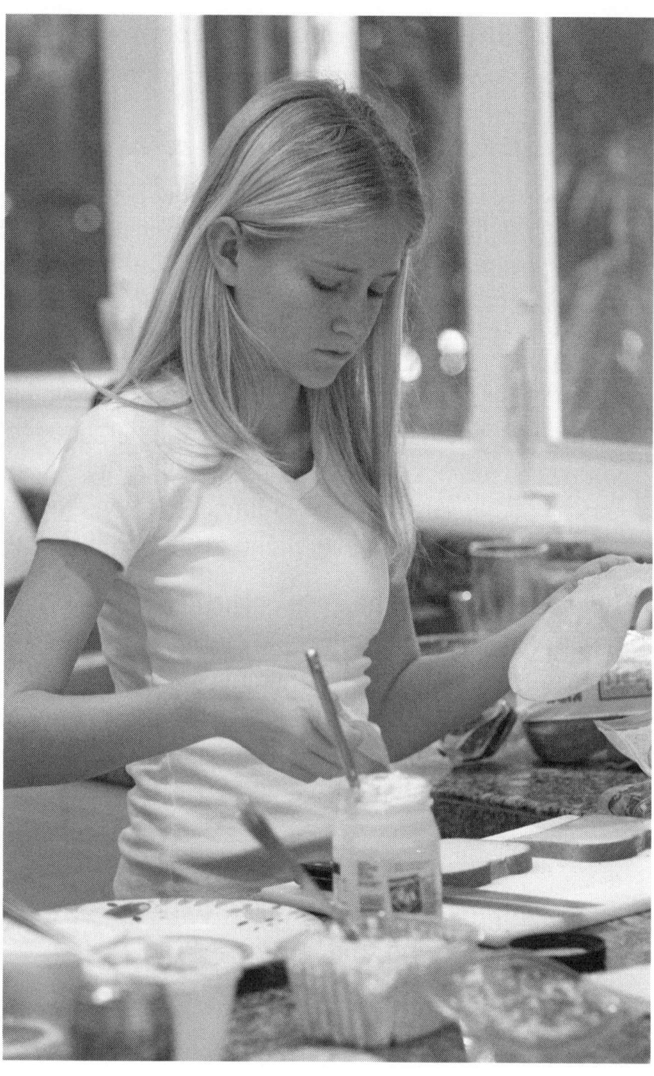

Useful language Imperatives

3 **Look back at Gina's email. Write the positive and negative imperatives that go before these words.**

1 *Try* writing down
2 ______ spend money
3 ______ sweets every day
4 ______ for five £1 coins
5 ______ realistic

4 **Put the words in order to make sentences.**

1 saving / every / Try / week / something
Try saving something every week.
2 extra money / work / Do / at home / some / to earn
______
3 things / Don't / silly / money / on / spend
______
4 extra money / things / Try / to get / selling
______
5 borrow / friends / from / Don't / your / money
______

Writing

WRITING TIP

Make it better! ✓✓✓
Use *and*, *or*, *but* and *so* to make your sentences longer.
I buy sweets ***and*** *chocolate.*
I earn lots of money ***but*** *I spend it all!*
I'd like to go to Australia ***so*** *I'm saving my pocket money.*

5 Complete the sentences with *and, or, but,* or *so*.

1 Don't spend all your pocket money ___*so*___ you can save some every week.
2 Don't buy sweets, water ________ sandwiches.
3 Make your own sandwich ________ bring your own water.
4 Try selling some books ________ CDs.
5 I get £5 a week ________ I spend it all!

6 Complete the sentences with the correct preposition.

1 Don't spend a lot of money ___*on*___ sweets.
2 Ask ________ your pocket money in coins.
3 Don't borrow money ________ your friends.
4 Would you like to sell this ________ me?
5 I'm trying to save money ________ my holidays.

WRITING TIP

Make it better! ✓✓✓
If a friend has a problem, say you understand and wish them good luck.
I understand your problem. Best of luck with it.

7 Read the sentences. Which ones say you understand (*U*) and which wish someone good luck (*GL*)?

1 I hope this works for you. *GL*
2 I totally understand the problem. ___
3 That happens to me too! ___
4 Best of luck. ___
5 I wish you luck. ___

8 Read Gina's email again and tick (✓) the information she includes.

Things not to do ☑
A friendly comment to start the email ☐
A nice way to finish the email ☐
Own experience ☐
Suggestions about what to do ☐
Asking for more information ☐
A reason why something is/isn't a good idea ☐

PLAN

9 Read the question in the email below. Use the information in Exercise 8 and make notes.

Hi everyone,
I want to earn some money for my summer holidays.
I need some ideas!
Thanks,
Freddie.

WRITE

10 Write an email. Look at page 17 of the Student's Book to help you.

____
____
____
____
____
____
____
____
____
____
____
____

CHECK

11 Check your writing. Can you say YES to these questions?

- Is the information from Exercise 8 in your description?
- Do you start by saying you understand and end by wishing them luck?
- Are there positive and negative imperatives?
- Do you join sentences with *and, or, but* or *so*?
- Do you use the correct prepositions?
- Are the spelling and punctuation correct?

Do you need to write a second draft?

1 Review

Vocabulary
Shops

1 Circle the correct options.

1 A bookshop sells **books** / **sweets**.
2 A chemist sells **medicine** / **newspapers**.
3 A newsagent sells **shoes** / **comics**.
4 A sports shop sells **trainers** / **books**.
5 A music shop sells **guitars** / **computers**.
6 An electronics shop sells **laptops** / **CDs**.
7 A supermarket sells **food and drink** / **pianos**.
8 A shoe shop sells **posters** / **shoes**.
9 A department store **has got** / **hasn't got** electronics.
10 A clothes shop sells **shirts** / **cheese**.

Total: 9

Money verbs

2 Complete the text with the verbs in the box.

spend save earn ~~sell~~ buy borrow

I want to [1] *sell* my old computer and [2] ________ a new one. I [3] ________ some of my money every week because I don't usually [4] ________ all of my pocket money. At the weekend, I [5] ________ money doing jobs in the garden for our neighbours. I can also [6] ________ some money from my mum and pay it back later.

Total: 5

Language focus
Present continuous

3 Complete the conversation with the present continuous form of the verbs in the box.

drink leave not answer not work buy ~~wait~~ walk eat

Joe: Where are you? We [1] *'re waiting* for you in the café.
Tom: I [2] ________ a CD for you.
Joe: That's nice of you! Thanks! I [3] ________ hot chocolate at the moment and Sarah [4] ________ a cake.
Tom: Where's Peter? He [5] ________ his phone.
Joe: That's because his phone [6] ________ . He's here. He [7] ________ into the café right now.
Tom: Great! I [8] ________ the shop now. See you in a bit.

Total: 7

Present simple vs. continuous

4 Complete the text with the correct form of the verbs in brackets.

I usually [1] *go* (go) shopping with my friends on Saturdays. My sister [2] ________ (not go) with us. She usually [3] ________ (go) to her friend's house. But today we [4] ________ (not go) anywhere. We [5] ________ (stay) at home. My sister [6] ________ (make) a cake. I [7] ________ (write) in my blog and Mum [8] ________ (listen) to music. We [9] ________ (not spend) a lot of time together at home. We sometimes [10] ________ (talk) to each other only by phone or text! So today we [11] ________ (do) something different. It's a nice change!

Total: 10

(don't) want to, would(n't) like to, would prefer to

5 Complete the sentences with *want*, *like* or *prefer*.

1 **A:** Do you *want* to go shopping?
B: I don't like shopping. I'd ________ to play volleyball.
2 **A:** Would you ________ to go cycling on Saturday?
B: No, I ________ to stay at home and play video games.
3 **A:** Do you ________ to save money?
B: Yes, but I'd also ________ to buy a new computer!
4 **A:** I think I'd ________ to sell my bicycle.
B: Great because I ________ to buy it!
5 **A:** I haven't got enough money. I'd ________ to borrow some from you but I'd ________ not to pay it back until next month.
B: What? No way!

Total: 9

(not) enough + noun

6 Complete the sentences with *enough* and the words in the box.

people money ~~food~~ cheese homework time

1 I want to make lunch for my friends but we haven't got *enough food* .
2 My parents would like to go snowboarding this year but they haven't got ___________ .
3 I need to call my grandma this morning but I haven't got ___________ .
4 We'd like to start a school volleyball team but we haven't got ___________ .
5 Have we got ___________ to make a pizza?
6 The teacher is angry because the students don't do ___________ .

Total: 5

Language builder

7 Circle the correct words.

Gina: I [1]___________ my new trainers today. Do you [2]___________ them?
Chris: They're great. I need [3]___________ trainers. Where [4]___________ them?
Gina: I [5]___________ them online. How about you?
Chris: I [6]___________ to the sports shop in town. I [7]___________ in town on Saturdays and there's a shop on my way home.
Gina: Have you got [8]___________ pairs of trainers?
Chris: Only two. I haven't got [9]___________ to buy more. I [10]___________ to buy another pair.
Gina: Me too!
Chris: But you [11]___________ a new pair!
Gina: Oh yeah!

1 **a** wear **(b)** 'm wearing
2 **a** likes **b** like
3 **a** some **b** any
4 **a** do you buy **b** you buy
5 **a** usually buy **b** buy usually
6 **a** sometimes go **b** go sometimes
7 **a** often am **b** am often
8 **a** much **b** many
9 **a** enough money **b** money enough
10 **a** like **b** 'd like
11 **a** wear **b** 're wearing

Total: 10

Vocabulary builder

8 Complete the table with the words in the box.

~~spend~~ newsagent bowling bookshop save borrow skiing chemist cycling yoga earn supermarket department store basketball buy skateboarding karate sell

Sports	Shops	Money verbs
		spend

Total: 17

Speaking

9 Circle the correct options.

Martina: Excuse me, [1](I'd like) / I like to buy a T-shirt.
Shop assistant: What [2]**size / number** are you?
Martina: I'm a small.
Shop assistant: What about this one?
Martina: I'd [3]**want / prefer** a red one.
Shop assistant: A red one? Here you [4]**be / are**.
Martina: Can I try it on?
Shop assistant: Yes, sure. … How is it?
Martina: It's great. How [5]**much / money** is it?
Shop assistant: It's €6.99.
Martina: [6]**I take / 'll take** it.

Total: 5

Total: 77

Get it right! Unit 1

Present simple vs. continuous

Remember that:

- we use the present simple to talk about facts, habits and routines.
- we use adverbs of frequency with the present simple.
- we use the present continuous to talk about actions in progress at the time of speaking.
- we use *at the moment* and *(right) now* with the present continuous.

1 Correct the incorrect sentences.

1 At the weekend, I'm often going shopping.
At the weekend, I often go shopping.

2 I'm helping Mum in the kitchen right now.
____

3 Alex isn't here – he visits a friend at the moment.
____

4 I've got some important news! Are you listening?
____

5 In my country, we are drinking a lot of tea.
____

(don't) want to, would(n't) like to, would prefer to

Remember that:

- we use the infinitive with *to* after ***want***, ***would like*** and ***would prefer***.
  ✓ *I **would like to go** shopping.*
  ✗ ~~*I would like going shopping.*~~
- we use ***would***, not *do*, to make questions with ***would like*** and ***would prefer***, but we use ***do*** to make questions with ***want***.
  ✓ ***Would you like** to come to the supermarket?*
  ✗ ~~*Do you like to come to the supermarket?*~~

2 Circle the correct words.

Jack: Hi, Emily. [1] **Do / Would** you like to come shopping with me? I want [2] **buy / to buy** some new clothes for my holiday.
Emily: OK. But I [3] **don't / not** want to go to the shopping centre in town. I [4] **would / will** prefer to go to the department store. It has better clothes.
Jack: OK. We can walk to the department store, or would you [5] **want / prefer** to go by bike?
Emily: Well, I think I'd like [6] **going / to go** by bike.
Jack: Is 3 o'clock OK? Or [7] **will / would** you prefer to go a bit later?
Emily: Yes, 3 o'clock is fine. See you then! Bye!

Extreme adjectives

Remember that:

- we use ***very*** to make adjectives stronger.
- we don't usually use ***very*** before extreme adjectives.
  ✓ *It's **very hot** in July, but in August it's **absolutely boiling**!*
  ✗ ~~*It's absolutely hot in July, but in August it's very boiling!*~~

3 Match the sentence halves.

1 Our holiday in England was absolutely … *f*
2 I'm watching the new *Batman* film. It's very … ___
3 Let's go to the beach. It's absolutely … ___
4 The new shopping centre is very … ___
5 My friend's new bedroom is absolutely … ___
6 Open the window. It's very … ___

a … big.
b … huge!
c … hot in here.
d … boiling!
e … good.
f … amazing!

Spell it right! The *-ing* form

Remember that:

- for verbs ending in *-e*, we remove the *e* before we add ***-ing***: give → **giving**.
- for verbs ending with one vowel and one consonant, we double the final consonant: shop → **shopping**.
- for verbs ending in *-y*, we just add *-ing*: study → **studying**.

4 Complete the sentences with the correct *-ing* form of the verb in brackets. Check your spelling!

1 We can't play football today. It's *raining* . (rain)
2 She's __________ a letter to her penfriend. (write)
3 We go __________ every day in the holidays. I love it! (swim)
4 I don't like __________ video games. Let's go outside. (play)
5 They enjoy __________ to music on their smartphones. (listen)
6 Kim and Julie are going __________ this afternoon. (shop)
7 They're __________ new clothes for their holidays. (buy)
8 They're __________ for their holiday in Greece. (save)

2 Our heroes

Vocabulary

Jobs

1 ★ Find nine more jobs in the word search.

a	s	t	m	u	m	o	t	e	r	l	w	a
c	w	r	u	b	j	u	p	i	b	d	l	s
r	e	i	s	y	o	l	k	s	e	a	n	t
p	o	l	i	c	e	o	f	f	i	c	e	r
a	l	o	c	n	g	v	f	i	l	t	m	o
d	a	f	i	t	r	e	c	r	y	o	k	n
l	i	n	a	k	u	t	h	e	s	r	t	a
w	e	s	n	u	r	s	e	f	m	o	n	u
o	d	f	b	n	u	l	s	i	e	v	e	t
c	a	h	t	r	i	w	e	g	o	p	e	r
i	n	p	o	l	r	v	e	h	a	c	r	e
s	c	i	e	n	t	i	s	t	n	o	r	s
j	e	y	o	n	e	c	h	e	r	t	h	l
q	r	z	u	i	m	x	a	r	t	i	s	t

2 ★★ Circle the correct words in the conversation.

A: What do you want to do when you leave school?

B: I want to be rich and famous! When I was little, I wanted to be an [1]**artist / astronaut** and travel to the moon, or a [2]**vet / nurse** and save animals' lives or work in a zoo!

A: Oh, so what are you good at?

B: Not a lot! I like acting, but I'm not very good and I can't play the guitar.

A: So you don't want to be a [3]**musician / firefighter** or [4]**an actor / a police officer**?

B: No! I don't think so. I don't think I'm very creative.

A: Well, what about a [5]**nurse / scientist** – then you can help people get better.

B: No, I think that's a difficult job. I'd really like to be [6]**an artist / a dancer** and paint beautiful pictures.

3 ★★★ Complete the definitions with the words from Exercise 1.

1 They move to music. You can see them in the theatre or at a concert. *dancer*
2 They find people who do bad things. ____________
3 They play the guitar, the piano or another instrument. ____________
4 You can see them in the theatre, on TV or in films. ____________
5 They work in a hospital, helping doctors. ____________
6 They paint pictures or make beautiful things. ____________
7 They help animals when they're sick. ____________
8 They travel to space and they sometimes stay there for a few months. ____________
9 They study and work in universities or laboratories. ____________
10 They help people when a building is on fire. ____________

4 ★★★ Choose two or three jobs. What is good about them? What isn't very good? Write at least five sentences.

It's a very interesting job. A scientist needs to study for a long time.

____

____

____

____

____

Language focus 1

was/were

1 ★ Circle the correct words.

1	I/He/She/It **was / were** there.
2	You/We/They **was / were** there.
3	I/He/She/It **wasn't / weren't** there.
4	You/We/They **wasn't / weren't** there.

2 ★★ Complete the sentences with *was* or *were* (✓), *wasn't* or *weren't* (✗).

1 We ___*were*___ (✓) both in the hockey team, but you ___________ (✓) a good player and I ___________ (✗) very good.

2 Bill Gates and Paul Allen ___________ (✗) interested in finishing their university studies. They ___________ (✓) only interested in computers.

3 Before he ___________ (✓) an actor, Hugh Jackman ___________ (✓) a PE teacher at a school.

4 Kaká ___________ (✓) always a good footballer and his brother, Digão, ___________ (✓) just like him. They ___________ (✓) both very good footballers but Kaká ___________ (✓) better.

Past simple: affirmative and negative

3 ★ Circle the correct words.

1	I/You/He/She/It/We/They **staying / stayed** there.
2	I/You/He/She/It/We/They **didn't stay / didn't stayed** there.
3	I/You/He/She/It/We/They **didn't go / didn't went** there.

4 ★★ Complete the newspaper story with the past tense form of the verbs in the box.

be not be ~~drop~~ not find go have not have look open phone pick say see take

Six months ago 15-year-old Courtney Barwick [1]___*dropped*___ her wallet outside a restaurant. When she got home, she [2]___________ for it in her bag, but it [3]___________ there. Courtney went to the restaurant, but she [4]___________ the wallet. She didn't expect to see it again, but she was lucky. Someone saw it, [5]___________ it up and [6]___________ it to a bank. The wallet [7]___________ Courtney's phone number in it, so the bank [8]___________ her to tell her they had her wallet. The next day, she [9]___________ to the bank to get it. When she [10]___________ the wallet, she [11]___________ $20 inside it, and a note. The note [12]___________ 'Surprise!' and it [13]___________ a surprise, because when Courtney lost her wallet, it [14]___________ any money in it!

5 ★★★ Your friend Paul lost something last week. Answer the questions with full sentences using the words in brackets.

1 What did he lose? (tablet)
He lost his tablet.

2 When did he lose it? (last Friday)
____

3 What happened? (leave / on the bus)
____

4 Did he find it again? How? (Yes / the driver / pick it up)
____

5 How did he get it back? (go / bus station / get it)
____

Time expressions

6 ★★ Order the sentences with time expressions. Start with the most recent.

a I went to the shop yesterday. ___

b I did my homework this morning. _1_

c They couldn't play the piano when they were little. ___

d My parents visited Rome four days ago. ___

e They went snowboarding last month. ___

Explore expressions with *make*

7 ★★ Match the sentence beginnings (1–6) with the sentence endings (a–f).

1 My homework was really bad _c_

2 I like cooking so I sometimes help ___

3 When I was at summer camp last year, ___

4 OK, you don't know what to do, ___

5 I want to do something amazing ___

6 Before you go out, ___

a I made lots of friends.

b so I can make history.

c because I made a lot of mistakes.

d so can I make a suggestion?

e make sure you do your homework.

f my mum to make a cake.

Listening and vocabulary

Adjectives of character

1 ★ **Use the clues to complete the crossword.**

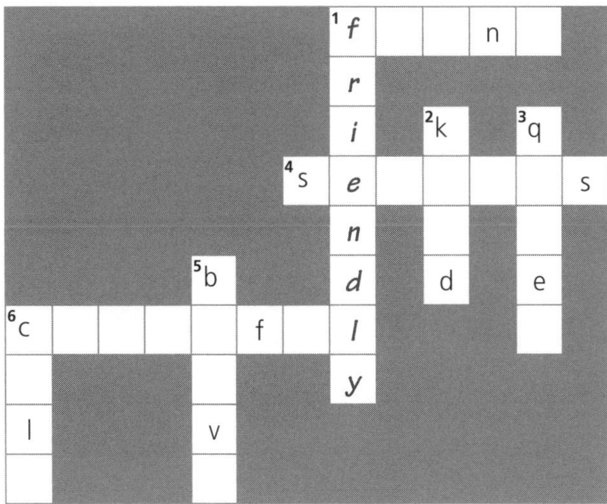

across

1 She always makes people laugh.

4 He didn't laugh or smile at all.

6 She is always happy and smiling.

down

1 The new student talked to lots of people.

2 He gave me some of his food.

3 Mark didn't say anything all evening.

5 Ellen wasn't afraid of the snake.

6 My friend never gets stressed.

2 ★★ **Circle the correct words.**

My two best friends are Chris and Adam. They are very different. Chris and I are always laughing because he is very [1]**funny / brave**, but Adam is very [2]**cheerful / serious**. He doesn't smile much. A lot of people think he is unhappy but he isn't, he's quite [3]**cheerful / kind** really! He is also a very [4]**brave / quiet** person, especially at school, where he doesn't talk much. Chris is the opposite. He's [5]**friendly / calm** to everyone and never stops talking! I'm not good at Science like they are, but they are both really [6]**kind / serious** and help me with my homework or before an exam. Last term I was nervous before a Physics exam! Chris and Adam never panic. They told me to be [7]**friendly / brave**, stay [8]**quiet / calm**, and do the exam. And they were right, it wasn't a difficult exam and I passed!

Listening

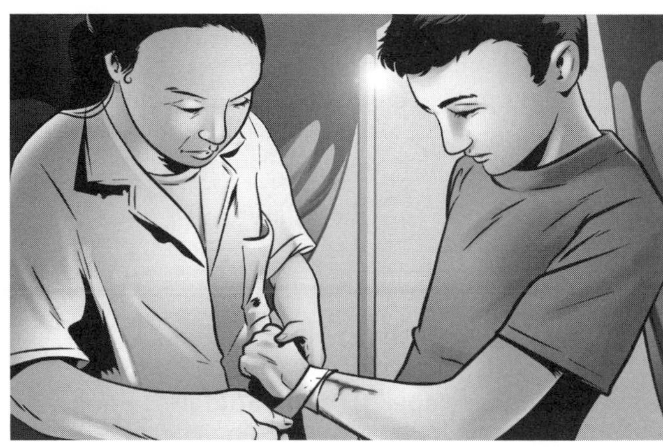

3 ★★ 02 **Listen to the radio interview with a teenager called Jonah. What happened to him? Circle the correct option.**

a He was ill on a survival course.

b He saved his friend from the river.

c He survived a bear attack.

4 ★★ 02 **Listen again. Circle the correct words.**

1 **Two / Three** teenagers were injured in a bear attack.

2 They were on a survival course in **Alaska / Australia**.

3 When the attack happened, the teenagers were **walking / camping**.

4 The accident happened **before / after** dinner.

5 When Jonah saw the bear, he **did / didn't do** what the instructors said.

6 The attack was very **fast / slow**.

7 The rescue helicopter arrived **that night / in the morning**.

8 Tracey Smith was **a teacher / a student** with the group.

Language focus 2

was/were: questions

1 ★ Complete the questions and short answers in the grammar table.

1 A: ___________ you at the concert last night? B: Yes, I ___________ .	
2 A: ___________ the bands good? B: No, they ___________ .	

2 ★★ Put the words in order to make questions. Then write the answers. You can check your answers on page 20 of the Student's Book.

1 Columbus / born / was / Where / ?
Where was Columbus born? In *Genoa* .

2 Anne Frank / during / was / the Second World War / Where?
___________ In ___________ .

3 Tim Berners-Lee's / What / job / was?
___________ He ___________

4 family / Anne Frank / and / Who / of / were / her / afraid?
___________ They ___________

5 was / Columbus / 1492 / Where / in?
___________ In ___________

6 the / What / of / Tim Berners-Lee's / name / was / invention?
___________ The ___________

Past simple: questions

3 ★★ Complete the questions to a teenager who sailed across the Atlantic alone. Use the question words and words in brackets to help you.

How long How many What ~~When~~ Where

1 *When did you decide* to sail across the Atlantic? (you/ decide)
Last year.

2 ___________ ? (the trip / take)
Seven weeks.

3 ___________ hours ___________ at night? (you / sleep)
Two or three.

4 ___________ a lot of sharks? (you / see)
Yes, and dolphins.

5 ___________ all day? (you / do)
I looked after the boat.

6 ___________ the trip? (you / finish)
In the Caribbean.

4 ★★★ Write questions in the past simple about the <u>underlined</u> information.

1 Marie Curie won <u>the Nobel Prize for Physics</u> in 1903.
What did Marie Curie win in 1903?

2 Christopher Columbus made his fourth and final voyage <u>in 1502</u>.
____

3 Anne Frank and her family lived in those small rooms <u>for two years</u>.
____

4 Tim Berners-Lee studied <u>at Oxford</u> from 1973 to 1976.
____

5 Marie Curie was born <u>in Poland</u> in 1867.
____

6 The USA <u>made Columbus Day a holiday</u> in 1937.
____

5 ★★★ Imagine you are interviewing Tim Berners-Lee. Read the answers and write the correct questions.

1 *Where were you born?*
I was born in England.

2 ___________
I studied Engineering at Oxford University.

3 ___________
I called it the *World Wide Web* because I knew it was for the whole world.

4 ___________
Oh, yes I made lots of mistakes – like the '//' in web addresses. It's really not necessary!

Explore the suffix *-ness*

6 ★ Circle the adjectives in the box that do <u>not</u> add *-ness* to make a noun.

sad favourite tidy kind funny
~~ill~~ brilliant happy big weak

7 ★★ Complete the sentences with words from Exercise 6.

1 His uncle has a very serious *illness* .

2 My teacher really likes the ___________ of my homework.

3 Thank you very much for your ___________ .

4 Brendan felt a great ___________ when his cat died.

5 Liam's very good at football – his only ___________ is his left foot.

6 My grandmother always said that ___________ was the most important thing in life.

Reading

The Heroes of BRITAIN

Every autumn a TV channel organises the Pride of Britain awards ceremony. The awards ***celebrate*** people who make the world a better place and ***inspire*** others. The winners are ordinary people, but they all did something extraordinary. The programme shows a special film about each winner. They are children, teenagers and adults, from six to 95 years old. The public, charities and the emergency services (firefighters, police, etc.) send in the names of people they want to win, and famous actors, politicians and singers present the awards.

Here are some recent winners:

Child of Courage:
TOM PHILLIPS, 9

When a bull attacked Tom's dad on their farm, Tom drove the farm ***tractor*** (for the first time!) at the bull and saved his dad's life.

Teenager of Courage:
JACK CARROLL, 14

Jack has cerebral palsy and needs a ***wheelchair***, but he still hopes to become a professional comedian. He first ***performed*** at a party for his parents, and then posted the video on YouTube. He often makes jokes about his ***disability***.

Great Bravery:
LUCY GALE, 33

Lucy, a taxi driver, saved two drivers after their cars crashed on a train crossing. She then moved one of the cars off the crossing seconds before an express train passed, and stopped a terrible train crash.

1 ★ **Read the text about a special TV programme. Tick (✓) the kind of people in the programme.**

actors and singers	☐	sportspeople	☐
children	✓	brave people	☐
teenagers	☐	heroes	☐

2 ★ **Look at the words in bold in the text. What kind of words (noun or verb) are they?**

1 celebrate *verb*
2 inspire ______
3 tractor ______
4 wheelchair ______
5 performed ______
6 disability ______

3 ★★ **Complete the definitions with the correct form of the words from Exercise 2.**

1 A person who can't walk needs a *wheelchair* .
2 A ______ is a large form of transport we use on a farm.
3 A ______ is an illness or injury that makes it difficult to do things other people can do.
4 Sometimes you want to do something because someone ______ you to do it.
5 When we say we admire someone and show them how much we like them, we ______ them.
6 When someone ______ , they tell other people stories or jokes, dance or play a musical instrument for them.

4 ★★ **Read the text again. (Circle) the correct answer for each question.**

1 When can you see the *Pride of Britain* awards ceremony?
(a) once a year b every four years c in the summer
2 What type of people win awards?
a famous actors b people who helped others c politicians
3 Who doesn't send in names of people to win the awards?
a the public b singers c police or ambulance workers
4 Who saved two people?
a Tom b Jack c Lucy
5 Who doesn't usually use anything with wheels?
a Tom b Jack c Lucy
6 Who wants to be famous one day?
a Tom b Jack c Lucy

5 ★★★ **Is there an award like the *Pride of Britain* in your country? Do you know about anyone who is an 'ordinary' hero? What did they do?**

Writing

A description of a person you admire

1 Read Patrick's description of a person he admires. Why was Judith by the river?

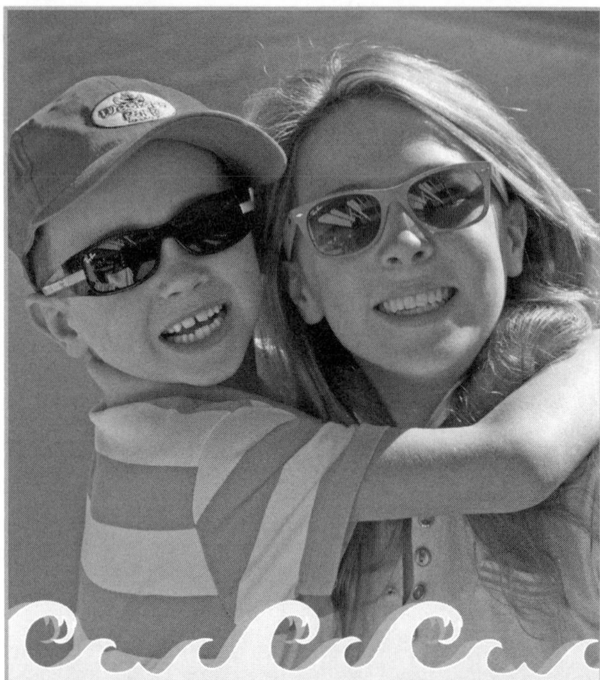

One person I admire is Judith, a girl who lives on my street. She's older than I am but she's in my sister's class and they're in the same swimming club as well.

She's got a dog so she often takes it for walks by the river at the back of our house. Last winter a small boy fell into the river and couldn't swim. Judith heard him scream and didn't stop to think. Although the water was very cold, she jumped in to rescue him. The boy disappeared under the water, but Judith stayed calm and pulled him out. A neighbour saw them and went to help them get out of the water. They were both fine after they got warm again.

I admire her because she saved the boy's life, but she says it was nothing special! She is very brave. The boy's parents think she is a hero and I agree.

2 Read the description again. Answer the questions.

1 How does Patrick know Judith? ________
2 Why did the boy scream? ________
3 What did Judith do? ________
4 What happened when they were in the water? ________
5 What does Judith think about what happened? ________

Useful language Connectors

3 Look back at the text. Which words does Patrick use to join these ideas? Where do they go in the sentence?

1 My sister and Judith are in the same class. They are in the same swimming club.
and (in the middle), as well (at the end)
2 She's got a dog. She often takes it for walks by the river.
____
3 The water was very cold. She jumped in to rescue him.
____
4 I admire her. She saved the boy's life.
____

4 Join the sentences using the connectors in brackets.

1 The bag was very heavy. He carried it for her. (although)
Although the bag was very heavy, he carried it for her.
2 We live in the same street. We go to the same school. (and, as well)
____
3 We both like music. We decided to start a band together. (so)
____
4 The man couldn't get up the stairs. He was in a wheelchair. (because)
____

5 Look back at the text. Find apostrophes and match them with their uses.

1 *She's* = She is
2 ________ = possession
3 ________ = they are
4 ________ = could not
5 ________ = She has

6 Write apostrophes in the correct place in the sentences.

1 They're my sister's best friends.
2 Shes a real hero because she saved the boys life.
3 Were in the same class so were the same age.
4 Life wasnt easy for her and she didnt have a lot of money.
5 Id like to be like him when Im older.

Writing

WRITING TIP

Make it better! ✓✓✓

Use the infinitive with *to* to explain the purpose of an action (why someone did something).

I went to the shop to buy some bread.

7 Complete the sentences with the infinitive form of the verbs in the box.

make become rescue ~~help~~ find out earn

1 She heard a girl shout so she ran *to help* her.
2 We called our friend ____________ what happened.
3 He studied very hard ____________ a doctor.
4 They worked very hard ____________ enough money.
5 He climbed the tree ____________ the cat.
6 Gary went slowly ____________ sure he didn't fall.

WRITING TIP

Make it better! ✓✓✓

Write about the person's character – use adjectives to say what the person is like.

My aunt can be quite serious but she's very kind, too.

8 Read the sentences. Which one does not describe someone's character?

1 She's really friendly and she talks to everyone.
2 Linda is kind and always finds time for her friends.
3 My uncle is very brave but he doesn't think so.
4 He's quite young and he's tall and strong.
5 Robbie always tells jokes – he's really funny.

9 Look back at Patrick's description. Order the things he talks about.

what other people think of him/her
~~who the person is~~ why you admire them
how you know the person what the person did
the person's character

1 *who the person is*
2 ____________
3 ____________
4 ____________
5 ____________
6 ____________

PLAN

10 Choose a person you know and admire to write about. Use the things in Exercise 9 and make notes.

WRITE

11 Write the description. Look at page 27 of the Student's Book to help you.

____

CHECK

12 Check your writing. Can you say YES to these questions?

- Is the information from Exercise 9 in your description?
- Do you describe the person's character and say why you admire them?
- Do you use connectors to join sentences?
- Do you use the infinitive with *to* to explain the purpose?
- Do you use apostrophes correctly?
- Are the spelling and punctuation correct?

Do you need to write a second draft?

2 Review

Vocabulary
Jobs

1 Match the words in the box with the jobs in the pictures.

dancer police officer musician actor nurse artist vet ~~astronaut~~ scientist firefighter

1 *astronaut* 2 ________ 3 ________ 4 ________

5 ________ 6 ________ 7 ________ 8 ________

9 ________ 10 ________

Total: 9

Adjectives of character

2 Circle the correct words.

1 I don't like going to the dentist. I'm not very **brave** / **friendly**.
2 Ellen usually laughs and smiles all day. She's very **funny** / **cheerful**.
3 Steven doesn't like talking. He's very **calm** / **quiet**.
4 Jessie always helps me with my homework. He's very **kind** / **stubborn**.
5 Jenny isn't nervous about exams. She's very **calm** / **serious**.
6 Max works hard at school. He's very **serious** / **brave**.
7 His stories always make me laugh. He's very **cheerful** / **funny**.

Total: 6

Language focus
was/were and past simple: affirmative and negative

3 Complete the sentences with the past form of the verbs in brackets.

1 I *was* born in Switzerland and I ________ to school in France. (be, go)
2 Bill ________ Science but he ________ good at languages. (study, not be)
3 Jane ________ around the world and ________ a book about her journey. (sail, write)
4 Maria ________ music but she ________ a famous singer. (not study, become)
5 Danny ________ good at art, but he ________ to be an artist. (be, not want)

Total: 9

Past simple: questions

4 Write a question for each answer.

1 **A:** Where / born?
Where were you born?
B: I was born in Italy.

2 **A:** What / study?
____
B: She studied Geography.

3 **A:** / good at sport?
____
B: No, they weren't good at sport.

4 **A:** / play tennis at school?
____
B: Yes, we did.

5 **A:** What / your book about?
____
B: My book was about mountain climbing.

Total: 4

Language builder

5 Choose the correct options.

Cheryl: What [1]______ yesterday? [2]______ you busy?
Jake: I [3]______ in the music shop on Saturday mornings. It [4]______ really busy on Saturdays.
Cheryl: Do you like [5]______ there?
Jake: Yes, I [6]______. But yesterday I [7]______ up late and then I [8]______ late for work.
Cheryl: Oh no!
Jake: The manager [9]______ very happy!
Cheryl: Do you play [10]______ musical instruments?
Jake: Yes, I [11]______ to play the guitar.

	a	b
1	a are you doing	(b) did you do
2	a Was	b Were
3	a work	b works
4	a is usually	b usually is
5	a work	b working
6	a am	b do
7	a got	b get
8	a am	b was
9	a wasn't	b weren't
10	a any	b much
11	a learn	b 'm learning

Total: 10

Vocabulary builder

6 Choose the correct options.

1 You can sometimes ______ extra pocket money by washing cars.
(a) earn b spend c borrow

2 A ______ studies Chemistry, Physics, or Biology.
a scientist b dancer c writer

3 You can usually buy magazines in ______ .
a a shoe shop b a newsagent c a clothes shop

4 Bill isn't scared. He's very ______ .
a serious b cheerful c brave

5 I'm trying to ______ money by not buying chocolate.
a spend b save c earn

6 ______ creates pictures and paintings.
a An actor b An artist c An astronaut

7 Nina helps other people. She is very ______ .
a serious b quiet c kind

8 You can buy medicine in ______ .
a an electronics shop b a sports shop c a chemist

Total: 7

Speaking

7 Complete the conversation with the words in the box.

look	may	That	~~think~~	maybe	sure

Luke: Who do you [1] *think* it is?
Oli: I'm not [2]______ . He [3]______ be a footballer.
Luke: No, he doesn't [4]______ very sporty.
Oli: OK, then [5]______ he's a singer.
Luke: [6]______ 's possible.

Total: 5

Total: 50

Get it right! Unit 2

was/were

1 Complete the text with *was* or *were*.

Yesterday, my mum [1] *was* at the shopping mall all afternoon. My dad and my brother [2] ______ at a football match. So I [3] ______ at home alone. I watched a couple of programmes on TV, but they [4] ______ boring. I texted my friends, Anna and Maria, but they [5] ______ both busy. I started my homework, but it [6] ______ too difficult.

Spell it right! Shopping words

Remember to spell these clothes and shopping words correctly.

shopping	~~shoping~~	trainers	~~trainners~~
bought	~~bougth~~	trousers	~~trausers~~
expensive	~~spensive~~	T-shirt	~~T-shir~~

was/were: questions

Remember that:

- we make questions with ***was/were*** before the subject.
  ✓ ***Were you*** *at home last night?*
  ✗ ~~*You were at home last night?*~~
- we make information questions with the *Wh-* question word + ***was/were*** + subject.
  ✓ ***Where were you*** *last night?*
  ✗ ~~*Where you were last night?*~~
- we make questions with *how many* + subject + ***was/were***.
  ✓ ***How many students were*** *in your class?*
  ✗ ~~*How many were students in your class?*~~

2 Read the sentences about a party. Write the correct questions. Use *was/were*.

1. I was at a party on Saturday night.
   Where were you on Saturday night ?
2. The party was at Mary's house.
   ______________________________ ?
3. No, I wasn't late. I arrived at 8 o'clock.
   ______________________________ ?
4. There were 20 people at the party.
   ______________________________ ?
5. Yes, Peter and his brother were at the party.
   ______________________________ ?
6. I was at the party for three hours.
   ______________________________ ?
7. Yes, all the people at the party were happy.
   ______________________________ ?

Jobs

Remember that:

- we use ***a*** or ***an*** to talk about a person who does a particular job.
  ✓ *My brother wants to be **a** firefighter.*
  ✗ ~~*My brother wants to be firefighter.*~~
- we use ***a*** before consonants and ***an*** before vowel sounds.

3 Read the text. Add *a* or *an* in the correct places.

My friend James has got two brothers. Their dad is ^*a* famous artist and their mum is vet. But the brothers don't want to be artists or vets. James wants to be actor because he loves the theatre. His brother, Paul, would like to be firefighter or astronaut, but he isn't tall enough, so he wants to be police officer. And his younger brother, Michael, loves music, but he can't be singer, because he can't sing. But he plays the piano very well, so, maybe he will be musician.

Expressions with *make*

Remember, some nouns have **make** before them, but other nouns have **do** before them.

✓ *I want to **make a cake** for my sister's birthday.*
✗ ~~*I want to do a cake for my sister's birthday.*~~
✓ *Police officers make sure people don't **do bad things**.*
✗ ~~*Police officers make sure people don't make bad things.*~~

4 Complete the sentences with *make* or *do*.

1. Arturo didn't *do* his homework yesterday.
2. I'd like to __________ a suggestion.
3. What job do you want to __________ when you leave school?
4. What sports do you __________ in your free time?
5. I want to __________ friends with new people from different countries.
6. They like speaking English, but they often __________ mistakes.
7. Sara is ill, so she can't __________ the exam.
8. She works hard and helps people because she wants to __________ a difference.

3 Strange stories

Vocabulary

Action verbs

1 ★ **Find seven more action verbs in the word search. Write them under the correct picture.**

t	h	r	o	w	o	s	f	h	e
f	a	l	l	o	v	e	r	i	g
c	h	a	u	c	o	r	c	d	k
a	k	t	j	e	s	g	h	e	p
t	p	r	u	n	a	w	a	y	s
c	l	i	m	b	m	t	s	e	c
h	e	i	p	o	n	e	e	i	o
g	e	t	y	o	p	l	h	s	c

1 *throw*

2 ______

3 ______

4 ______

5 ______

6 ______

7 ______

8 ______

2 ★★ **Complete the sentences with the past simple form of the verbs from Exercise 1.**

1 He *threw* the empty bottle in the bin.
2 I didn't see the bag on the floor so I ______ it.
3 They ______ their friend across the park.
4 The police ______ the thieves at the airport with all the money.
5 My sister ______ Mont Blanc last summer. It's 4,810m high!
6 When I saw the big dog, I ______ . It was enormous!
7 The thief ______ out of the window.
8 My little brother ______ my mobile phone under the sofa for a joke. It wasn't funny.

3 ★★★ **Complete the story with the correct form of the words in Exercise 1.**

Why did my English teacher [1] *chase* me around the school? There was no time to think. 'You can't [2] ______ me,' I said! I [3] ______ out of the window into the playground and [4] ______ away. I tried to jump over the PE teacher's bicycle but it was too high and I [5] ______ over and hurt my leg. I got up quickly, went to the car park and [6] ______ behind the French teacher's car. The English teacher [7] ______ on to the car next me and [8] ______ his books at me. He was shouting my name: 'Justin! Justin!' Then I woke up … in my English class. The teacher smiled at me and said, 'You fell asleep, Justin!'

4 ★★★ **Write five sentences with the verbs in Exercise 1 about you or someone you know.**

When I was six, I fell over some books in my bedroom.

______
______
______
______
______

Language focus 1

Past continuous

1 ★ **Complete the table.**

	I / he / she / it	you / we / they
+	I [1] *was* running away.	We [6] ____ hiding.
-	He [2] ____ running away.	They [7] ____ hiding.
?	[3] ____ she running away? Yes, she [4] ____ . No, she [5] ____ .	[8] ____ they hiding? Yes, they [9] ____ . No, they [10] ____ .

2 ★★ **Look at the picture and write sentences.**

When the object appeared in the sky …

1 … we / play / football in the garden
We were playing football in the garden.

2 … my friend / catch / a ball
______

3 … my sister / climb / a tree
______

4 … my mum / talk / to a friend on the phone
______

5 … a car / drive / down the street
______

6 … our dog / chase / the car
______

7 … my neighbour / cut / the grass
______

8 … the police officers / help / an old lady
______

Past continuous questions

3 ★★ **Complete the detective's questions with the words in the box and the past continuous. Then complete the short answers.**

the men / carry	you and your friends / play	~~the woman / wear~~	you / watch	the man / drive

1 *Was the woman wearing* glasses?
No, *she wasn't* .

2 ______ TV at nine o'clock?
Yes, ______ .

3 ______ a big box?
No, ______ .

4 ______ the car?
No, ______ . It was the woman.

5 ______ football?
Yes, ______ . In the park.

4 ★★★ **Write questions with the past continuous. Answer them for you.**

1 What / you / wear / yesterday?
What were you wearing yesterday?
I was wearing a red T-shirt and black jeans.

2 What / you / do / at eight o'clock / this morning?
______
______

3 Who / you / talk to / on the phone / all afternoon?
______
______

4 you / listen to music / an hour ago?
______
______

Explore expressions with *look*

5 ★★ **Match the sentence beginnings (1–5) with the sentence endings (a–e).**

1 Tom was looking after his little brother *c*
2 I was looking in the kitchen window ____
3 Lydia was looking for her mobile phone ____
4 We were looking at some photos ____
5 Some people say I look like my mum ____

a when we saw something really funny.
b when I saw my mum drop the cake.
c because his parents were at work.
d but other people say I look like my dad.
e when she found some money.

Listening and vocabulary

Adverbs of manner

1 ★ **Write the adverbs for the adjectives below.**

1 careful *carefully*
2 easy ______
3 good ______
4 happy ______
5 quick ______
6 quiet ______
7 bad ______
8 slow ______

2 ★★ **Complete the sentences with the adverbs from Exercise 1.**

1 The weather is bad so drive *slowly* .
2 We played very ______ so the other team won.
3 He saw a big elephant so he ran away ______ .
4 The mountain was very high so we walked up it ______ .
5 I did ______ in my exam because I studied a lot.
6 We spoke ______ so nobody could hear us.
7 I was listening to music quite ______ until I remembered my homework!
8 It wasn't a high wall so we climbed over it ______ .

3 ★★★ **Complete the sentences with the adverbs from Exercise 1.**

1 It wasn't difficult to pass the exam.
I passed the exam *easily* .
2 We didn't drive fast.
We drove ______ .
3 We weren't being noisy.
We were talking very ______ .
4 I'm not very good at playing the guitar.
I play the guitar ______ .
5 He wasn't sad when he was singing.
He was singing ______ .
6 They are very good at volleyball.
They play volleyball very ______ .

Listening

4 ★ 03 **Listen to Vicky talking to her friend Mel about a book. What kind of book is it? Circle the correct option.**

a an adventure book
b a travel book
c a science-fiction story

5 ★★ 03 **Listen again and choose the correct answers.**

1 Vicky said sorry because …
a she was late.
(b) she didn't go to Mel's house yesterday.
2 The name of the book was …
a *The Thief Lord.*
b *Cornelia Funke.*
3 It was a good book so Vicky …
a was reading until six o'clock.
b didn't stop until the end.
4 Prosper and Bo ran away …
a to stay together.
b to find their mother.
5 They went to Venice because …
a it was their mother's favourite place.
b they knew some children there.
6 The Thief Lord took things from …
a Barbarossa.
b people with a lot of money.
7 Vicky says she liked the story because it was …
a surprising.
b magical.
8 Vicky doesn't tell Mel the end of the story because …
a it's very complicated.
b she wants Mel to read the book.

Language focus 2

Past simple vs. continuous

1 ★ Match the parts of the sentences to make rules.

1. We use the past simple
2. We use the past continuous

a. to talk about an action that was in progress in the past.
b. to talk about a short, finished action in the past.

2 ★★ Circle the correct options in the story.

An Italian man [1] **looked / was looking** at a painting on the wall in his father's kitchen. The painting looked like something he once [2] **saw / was seeing** in a book about the famous French painter Paul Gauguin. His father [3] **told / was telling** him he found the painting many years ago on a train when he [4] **travelled / was travelling** to Paris. His son read about the painting on the Internet and [5] **found out / was finding out** that it was really a painting by Gauguin. The police discovered the interesting story behind the painting. A man [6] **went / was going to** an old lady's house to clean the windows. While the old lady [7] **made / was making** some tea, the man took the painting off the wall and [8] **left / was leaving** the house quietly. While he [9] **sat / was sitting** on the train, he realised he [10] **didn't know / wasn't knowing** what to do with the painting so he left it carefully on the seat.

could(n't)

3 ★ Complete the sentences with the words in the box.

could past couldn't subject

1. We use *could* and *couldn't* + infinitive without *to* to talk about ability in the ________ .
2. Questions: *Could* + ________ + infinitive?
3. Short answers: Yes, she ________ . No, they ________ .

4 ★★ Complete the conversation with *could* or *couldn't*.

A: What's the Loch Ness monster?
B: Well, in Scotland there's a lake called Loch Ness. They say a monster lives in the lake but nobody [1] *could* find it.
A: Why do they think there's a monster in the lake?
B: Well, someone took a photo in 1937. In the photo you [2] ________ see a long neck and a head above the water. And there's a video from 2007 as well. A man said he [3] ________ see something long and black in the water but he [4] ________ see what it was. Scientists spent many years looking in the lake but they [5] ________ find anything.
A: Are there any other photos of it?
B: Well, a man was looking at maps on his computer in 2014 and said he [6] ________ see something in a photo of the lake.
A: I'd like to go there.
B: You [7] ________ go there because it's in Scotland and you hate the cold!

Past simple, past continuous and *could*

5 ★★★ Read the conversation and write questions with the past simple, past continuous or *could*.

Policeman:	[1] *What were you doing when you saw the light?*
Man:	I was driving.
Policeman:	[2] ________
Man:	Because I was going home.
Policeman:	[3] ________
Man:	Well, I couldn't see much, only a very big object and bright lights.
Policeman:	[4] ________
Man:	No, I didn't see anyone else.

Explore nouns with *-er*

6 ★★ Write the names of the people with *–er*.

1. I live on an island. *islander*
2. I take photos. ________
3. I work on a farm. ________
4. I explore new places. ________
5. I build things. ________
6. I'm shopping. ________
7. I'm swimming. ________
8. I paint. ________

Reading

1 ★ Read the article. What was in the water?

A plane CRASH?

In March 2014, islanders on Gran Canaria were looking at the sea when they saw a big yellow object. It was long, with a yellow tail and it was in the water near the **coast**. They called the emergency services – the police, ambulances and the coast guard.

The emergency services told the newspapers that a plane was in the Atlantic Ocean about one kilometre from the coast of Gran Canaria.

At about 3 pm, the BBC and other TV channels around the world began to **report** that a Boeing 737 **crashed** into the sea. Workers in the **control tower** at the airport in Gran Canaria **confirmed** the reports: 'We are missing a plane!' one airport worker said. Another plane that was flying over the area also saw the plane in the water.

A helicopter and a boat went out to sea to rescue the passengers but when they arrived, they found nothing. There was only a large tugboat – a boat that pulls other boats across the sea.

Finally, the emergency services confirmed the **false alarm**. It was not a plane – just a boat that looked a bit like a plane. Nobody knows what happened to the 'missing plane' from the airport!

2 ★★ Match the words in bold with the definitions.

1 A building at an airport where they watch planes. *control tower*
2 To say that something was definitely true. ______
3 The land near the sea. ______
4 When someone thinks something is going to happen but it doesn't. ______
5 Give information about something. ______
6 When a car, plane or train hits something else. ______

3 ★★★ Read the text again and put the events in the correct order.

a They found a tugboat. ___
b They called the emergency services. ___
c A helicopter and a boat went to the plane. ___
d TV channels said a plane was in the sea. ___
e People saw a plane in the sea. *1*
f Airport workers said a plane was missing. ___

4 ★★★ Do you know any stories about false alarms? Can you invent one? Write five sentences.

______
______
______
______
______

Writing

A story

1 Read the story. What did Mr James do?

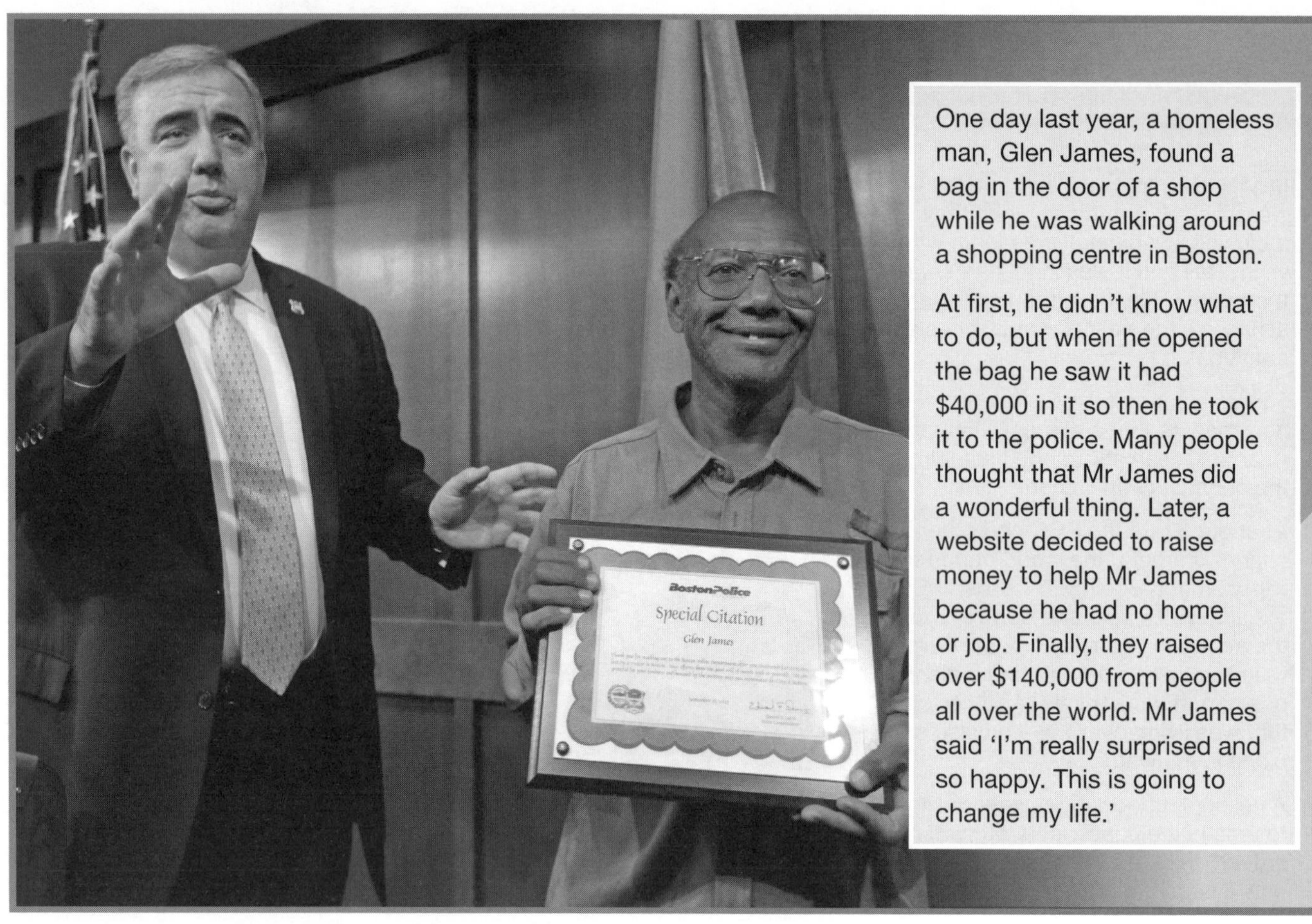

One day last year, a homeless man, Glen James, found a bag in the door of a shop while he was walking around a shopping centre in Boston.

At first, he didn't know what to do, but when he opened the bag he saw it had $40,000 in it so then he took it to the police. Many people thought that Mr James did a wonderful thing. Later, a website decided to raise money to help Mr James because he had no home or job. Finally, they raised over $140,000 from people all over the world. Mr James said 'I'm really surprised and so happy. This is going to change my life.'

2 Read the story again. Answer the questions.

1 What was Glen James doing when he found the bag? ________
2 What was in the bag? ________
3 Who did Mr James give the bag to? ________
4 How much did the website raise for Mr James? ________

Useful language **Sequencing language 1**

3 Look back at the story. Find sequencing words and phrases.

1 O*ne day*________
2 w________
3 A___ f________
4 w________
5 t________
6 L________
7 F________

4 Complete the story with the words and phrases from Exercise 3.

[1] *One day* last summer a woman was walking in the park [2]________ she found a lost dog. [3]________ , she didn't know what to do because she had a sick child. She didn't think she could look after a dog and a child, so she put a poster up in her village, but nobody came to collect the dog. [4]________ , one afternoon [5]________ she was working in her garden, the dog started to make lots of noise. She followed it into the kitchen and found her son on the floor. [6]________ , the doctors said her son almost died but the dog saved him before it was too late. [7]________ , the woman decided to keep the dog because it saved her son's life.

5 Be careful with the spelling of the past simple. Write the past simple forms of these verbs.

1 go *went*
2 be ________ ________
3 have ________
4 get ________
5 buy ________
6 try ________
7 drive ________
8 give ________
9 find ________
10 catch ________

Writing

WRITING TIP

Make it better! ✓✓✓
Describe your (or the other person's) reaction or feeling when something happens.
I was really surprised when I heard the news about Grandma.

6 **Complete the sentences with the words in the box.**

sad frightened happy angry ~~surprised~~

1 When I saw the huge present, I was very *surprised* .
2 He's ___________ because his brother broke his new tablet.
3 When my cat died, I felt really ___________ .
4 I was really ___________ because, finally, I found my mobile phone.
5 When he saw the snake, he was very ___________ .

7 **Read the story in Exercise 4 again and make notes about the information in the table.**

when the story happened	*last year*
where the story happened	
people in the story	
what they were doing	
events of the story	
how the story ended	
the people's feelings in the story	

PLAN

8 **Read the titles for a story below and choose one you like. Use the table in Exercise 7 and make notes. You can use your imagination or write about a true story.**

WRITE

9 **Write the story. Look at page 39 of the Student's Book to help you.**

____
____
____
____
____
____
____
____
____
____
____
____

CHECK

10 **Check your writing. Can you say YES to these questions?**

- Is the information from Exercise 9 in your description?
- Do you describe your/the person's reaction or feelings?
- Do you use sequencing words to order the events in the story?
- Do you spell the past simple forms correctly?

Do you need to write a second draft?

3 Review

Vocabulary
Action verbs

1 Circle the correct options.

1 The thief **jumped / threw** out of the window.
2 The burglars **hid / climbed** over a wall.
3 A neighbour **ran / chased** the thief into the garden.
4 The thief **fell over / threw** and broke her arm.
5 He **caught / hid** the money in a tree.
6 He **threw / chased** the newspaper in the bin.

Total: 5

Adverbs of manner

2 Put the letters in order to make adjectives. Change them to adverbs to complete each sentence.

1 I looked *carefully* for my keys. (farlecu)
2 It was cold so I walked home ________ . (kuqic)
3 We found the address ________ . (saye)
4 We lost because we weren't playing ________ . (ogdo)
5 The baby is sleeping, so please talk ________ . (tiqeu)
6 It's Sam's birthday and he is singing ________ . (pypah)
7 Tina was very tired so she cycled ________ . (oswl)
8 I did very ________ in the exam. My parents were angry. (dba)

Total: 7

Language focus
Past continuous

3 Complete the interview with the correct form of the past continuous.

Detective: [1] *Were* you *watching* (watch) from the window?
Peter: Yes, I [2]________ .
Detective: What [3]________ the men ________ (wear)?
Peter: One man [4]________ (wear) a brown jacket.
Detective: [5]________ he ________ (carry) anything?
Peter: Yes, he [6]________ (carry) a black bag.
Detective: [7]________ the men ________ (run)?
Peter: No, they [8]________ , but they [9]________ (walk) quickly.

Total: 8

Past simple vs. past continuous

4 Circle the correct options.

1 We **ate / were eating** dinner when the lights **went / were going** off.
2 We **slept / were sleeping** when the thieves **broke / were breaking** into the house.
3 One thief **fell / was falling** over while he **ran / was running** away.
4 The police **found / were finding** the money while they **searched / were searching** the garden.
5 One thief **drove / was driving** away in a car while the police **didn't look / weren't looking**.

Total: 9

could(n't)

5 Look at the pictures of Tom and complete the sentences with *could* or *couldn't* and the correct verb.

When Tom was five, he [1] *could read* stories, but he [2]________ . He [3]________ a bike without any problems and he was very musical so he [4]________ the guitar very well when he was ten, but he [5]________ the piano. Now he's 14 and he can do all of these things. What about you?

Total: 4

Vocabulary builder

6 Circle the correct words.

1 After school, Danny ___________ judo.
a goes (b) does c plays

2 I'm ___________ because I want to buy a new phone.
a saving b selling c spending

3 I sometimes buy this magazine at the ___________.
a chemist b shoe shop c newsagent

4 Larry talks to everybody. He's very ___________.
a calm b kind c friendly.

5 I love animals so I'd like to be a ___________.
a vet b actor c nurse

6 A man ___________ over the wall into our garden.
a chased b climbed c caught

7 I did my homework ___________ so I didn't make mistakes.
a carefully b easily c badly

8 He's got three cameras. He looks ___________ a photographer.
a for b after c like

9 When he saw the police officers, he ___________ so they couldn't find him.
a threw b hid c fell over

10 I ___________ listening to music in my room last night.
a were b was c am

Total: 9

Language builder

7 Circle the correct words.

Kim: [1]___________ you watch the detective show on TV last night? It [2]___________ really good!
Bill: No, I [3]___________ my homework. I [4]___________ a test this morning. But I love detective shows. What [5]___________ it about?
Kim: A group of thieves stole [6]___________ diamonds and the police [7]___________ understand how they did it.
Bill: What [8]___________ in the end?
Kim: I don't know. The final episode is on this evening. Do you want to watch it together?
Bill: OK!

1 a Do (b) Did c Were
2 a was b were c did
3 a did b was doing c am doing
4 a was having b was c had
5 a were b was c did
6 a much b any c some
7 a weren't b couldn't c aren't
8 a happened b happen c was happening

Total: 7

Speaking

8 Complete the conversation with the words in the box.

next do ~~strange~~ weird did What

A: Something [1] *strange* happened yesterday.
B: Really? [2]___________ ?
A: Well, I was walking home through the park.
B: What happened [3]___________ ?
A: I fell over but I don't know how it happened. And then a boy was standing next to me and he helped me to stand up.
B: What [4]___________ you say?
A: Well, I said thanks, of course.
B: What did you [5]___________ ?
A: I picked up my bag and when I stood up, the boy was gone. There was nobody in the park.
B: That's [6]___________ !

Total: 5

Total: 54

Get it right! Unit 3

Past simple vs. past continuous

Remember that:

- we use ***was*** or ***were*** + ***-ing*** to talk about an action that was in progress in the past.
  ✓ *The dog **was chasing** the cat.*
  ✗ ~~*The dog chasing the cat.*~~
- we use the past simple to talk about completed events and actions in the past. We never use ***was*** or ***were*** + past simple.
  ✓ *The dog **chased** the cat.*
  ✗ ~~*The dog was chased the cat.*~~
- we usually use ***while*** with the past continuous and ***when*** with the past simple.
  ✓ *The dog was chasing the cat **when** the man appeared.*
  ✗ ~~*The dog chased the cat while the man was appearing.*~~

1 Circle the correct words.

New mail

Dear Martin,

We went to the beach last weekend. Three of my cousins [1] were came / came with us. And our dog, Charlie, of course! It [2] rained / was raining when we left the house, but while we [3] driving / were driving there, the rain stopped. At first, everybody [4] was wanting / wanted to do different things. My parents wanted to sit and read. My cousins [5] were decided / decided to go swimming in the sea. We really [6] enjoyed / were enjoyed our day at the beach.

I hope you had a good weekend, too,

Jamie

could(n't)

Remember that:

- we use the infinitive without *to* after ***could(n't)***.
  ✓ *The test was easy. I **could answer** all the questions.*
  ✗ ~~*The test was easy. I could to answer all the questions.*~~
- we never use the past simple after ***could(n't)***.
  ✓ *They **couldn't open** the door.*
  ✗ ~~*They couldn't opened the door.*~~
- we use ***could(n't)***, not *can('t)*, to talk about ability in the past.
  ✓ *I'm sorry you **couldn't** come to my house yesterday.*
  ✗ ~~*I'm sorry you can't come to my house yesterday.*~~

2 Are the sentences correct? Correct the incorrect sentences.

1 I can't go to the cinema last night because I was looking after my sister.
I couldn't go to the cinema last night because I was looking after my sister.

2 I could hear the music but I couldn't see who was playing it.
____

3 It was great to see you. I'm so happy that you could to come.
____

4 We couldn't went to the beach because it was raining.
____

5 In the past, you couldn't to travel from London to Paris by train.
____

6 The exam was very difficult. I can't understand the questions.
____

Adjectives or adverbs?

Remember that:

- we use an adverb to describe a verb or an action.
  ✓ *He looked **carefully** at the picture.*
  ✗ ~~*He looked careful at the picture.*~~
- we use an adjective after ***be*** with an imperative.
  ✓ ***Be careful**! That water is very hot.*
  ✗ ~~*Be carefully! That water is very hot.*~~

3 Complete the sentences with a word from the box. Change the adjective to an adverb if necessary.

good	easy	quiet	careful	quick	bad	~~loud~~

1 There was a woman speaking *loudly* on her mobile phone.
2 They speak English very ____________ because their mother is English.
3 Be ____________ ! I'm trying to study.
4 He plays the piano very ____________ . It sounds awful!
5 Did you listen ____________ to what the teacher said?
6 I did my homework ____________ because I wanted to go to the cinema.
7 He climbed the wall ____________ because he's very tall.

Vocabulary

Things in the home

1 ★ **Look at the pictures of the things in the home. Write the words in the correct column. Some words can go in more than one column.**

living room	bedroom	bathroom	other rooms
	mirror	*mirror*	

2 ★★ **Complete the sentences with the words from Exercise 1.**

1 Where's my dictionary? It isn't on my *desk* or on the ______ with the other books.
2 My dad has two ______ on his bed because he says it's comfortable but I only have one.
3 In winter, I always sleep with a big ______ to keep warm.
4 Houses in the UK usually have ______ on the floor.
5 My little sister can't see herself in our bathroom ______ because she's too short.
6 My mum and dad have got a lot of clothes so their ______ is full.
7 Can you get the sugar? It's in the ______ in the kitchen.
8 When I wake up in the morning, I open the ______ and look outside.

3 ★★★ **Mark and Jane are in their new house but it's empty. Read the sentences and write what they need to buy.**

1 'We haven't got anywhere to put our clothes!' *wardrobe*
2 'There's nothing on the floor and it's very cold.' ______
3 'We've got plates and glasses for the kitchen but nowhere to put them.' ______
4 'I just washed my hands but I can't dry them.' ______
5 'Our neighbours can see us through the windows!' ______
6 'We've got nothing on the bed.' ______, ______
7 'I need a place to work and somewhere to put my books.' ______, ______
8 'I can't believe we can't wash the plates and glasses!' ______

4 ★★★ **What's your favourite room in your home? Why do you like it? What furniture does it have? What other furniture would you like to have? Write at least five sentences.**

My favourite room is my bedroom. I like it because it's a big, sunny room.

Language focus 1

Comparatives and superlatives

1 ★ **Complete the rules in the grammar table.**

-ier worse more (x2) Better ~~two~~ *-er*

1	We use comparative adjectives to compare *two* or more people, things, etc.
2	To form the comparative of short adjectives (one syllable) we add ________ .
3	To form the comparative of long adjectives (two syllables +) we use ________ before the adjective.
4	When the adjective has two syllables and ends in *-y*, we remove the *-y* and add ________ to form the comparative.
5	________ (good) and ________ (bad) are irregular comparatives.
6	To make the comparative form of an adverb we usually add ________ .

2 ★★ **Write comparative sentences.**

1 The Empire State Building / high / the Eiffel Tower
The Empire State Building is higher than the Eiffel Tower.
2 Buckingham Palace / big / the White House
3 His desk / expensive / all our furniture
4 A bed / comfortable / a sofa
5 The hotel in Santiago / good / the hotel in Buenos Aires
6 Gail's room / tidy / Kerry's

3 ★ **Choose the correct options to complete the grammar table.**

1	To form the superlative of short adjectives (one syllable) we add *-er* / *-est*
2	To form the superlative of long adjectives (two syllables +) we use *more* / *most* before the adjective.
3	When the adjective has two syllables and ends in *-y*, we remove the *-y* and add *-est* / *-iest* to form the superlative.
4	*Best* / *The best* and *worst* / *the worst* are irregular superlatives.

4 ★ **Complete the text with the superlative form of the adjectives in the box.**

big expensive ~~rich~~ tall ugly unusual

The billionaire Mukesh Ambani is [1]*the richest* man in India. He and his family live in a house called Antilia, in Mumbai, India. Antilia cost one billion dollars! It's [2]________ house in the world – a tower with 27 floors. It's also [3]________ family home in the world. There are three floors of gardens and it has [4]________ garage in a family house too, with space for 168 cars, all for Mr Ambani's family of six! Antilia is modern, but it isn't beautiful. In fact, many people think it's [5]________ building in Mumbai. I'm not sure about that, but it's probably [6]________ billionaire's house in the world!

5 ★★★ **Write the sentences in the comparative or superlative.**

1 Mount Everest / high / mountain / in the world
Mount Everest is the highest mountain in the world.
2 This pillow / soft / that pillow
3 The library / quiet / place in the school
4 The beach / relaxing / place to go in the summer
5 A holiday in New York / good / a holiday at home
6 My dad's car / small / my mum's car

Explore expressions with *do*

6 ★★ **Match the sentence beginnings (1–6) with the sentence endings (a–f).**

1 Could you do me a favour? *c*
2 Can I help you with your homework? ___
3 My dad can't play football with me ___
4 I didn't go out on Saturday because ___
5 Paul was really tired last night because ___
6 We put all the food in the cupboard ___

a I was doing my homework all day!
b after we did the shopping.
c Could you give me that book on the shelf?
d because he's doing the housework.
e he did sport for three hours.
f I like doing Maths.

Listening and vocabulary

Household appliances

1 ★ **Add vowels to make words for household appliances. Write them under the correct picture.**

dshwshr frzr rn ~~frdg~~ wshng mchn lmp hrdryr ckr htr

  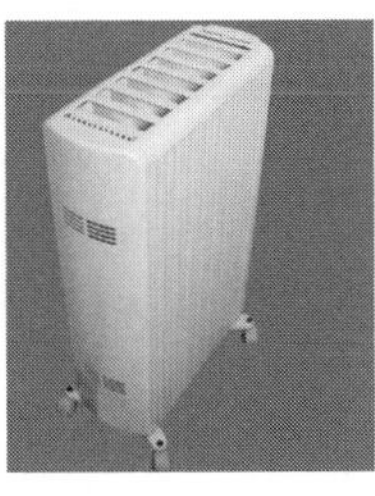

1 _fridge_ 2 ______ 3 ______

  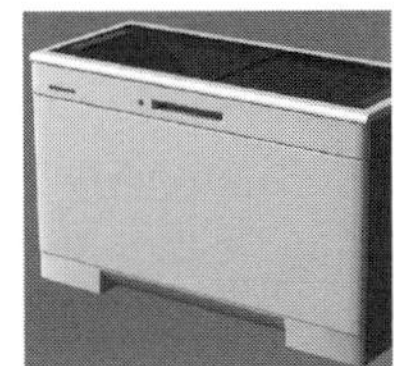

4 ______ 5 ______ 6 ______

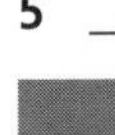 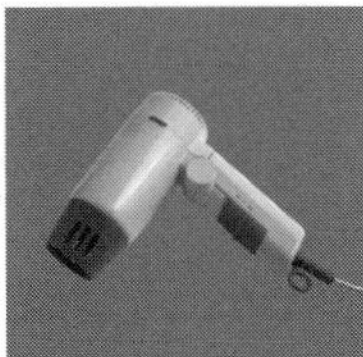 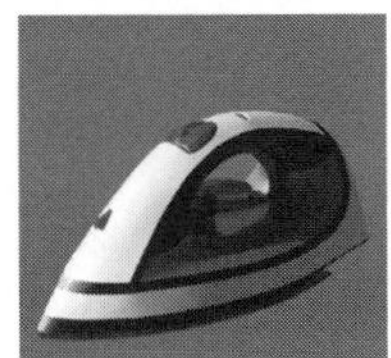

7 ______ 8 ______ 9 ______

2 ★★ **Match the words from Exercise 1 with the sentences.**

1 You use this when your hair is wet. _hairdryer_
2 This washes your clothes. ______
3 It keeps food cool and safe to eat. ______
4 It helps you see in the dark. ______
5 You use this when your house is cold. ______
6 It cleans the plates and glasses. ______
7 It makes your clothes look nice. ______
8 You use this to cook your dinner. ______
9 You can leave food in it for a long time. ______

3 ★★★ **Complete the text with the words from Exercise 1.**

The room with the most appliances in our house is the kitchen. I use the [1] _cooker_ every evening to make dinner.

We also use the [2] ______ once a day to wash our clothes, and the [3] ______ every day to clean the plates.

Of course, we always use the [4] ______ to keep our food cool and fresh. When my mum cooks, she often puts extra food in the [5] ______ . She says it can stay there for months. One thing I never use is the [6] ______. My mum hates this too, so my dad uses it for his shirts and my T-shirts.

Another thing I use every day is the [7] ______ on my desk – it helps me to see my books because my room is quite dark. And when it's cold, I sometimes use the [8] ______ to stay warm! I've got long hair so I also use my [9] ______ every day.

Listening

4 ★ 04 **Listen to the conversation between Ella and Nick. What are they talking about?**

5 ★★ 04 **Listen again. Mark the sentences true (*T*) or false (*F*).**

1 Ella and Nick are brother and sister. _T_
2 They went to see three flats. ___
3 One flat is really old. ___
4 Both flats had two bathrooms. ___
5 Ella likes the first flat better. ___
6 Nick and Ella usually catch the bus to school. ___
7 Their mum and dad want to plan a new bedroom. ___
8 Nick isn't sure the flat is big enough. ___

Language focus 2

must/mustn't, should/shouldn't

1 ★ Circle the correct words.

1 We use *must, mustn't, should* and *shouldn't* + verb / *to* + verb.
2 We use ***must / mustn't*** to talk about obligation.
3 We use ***must / mustn't*** to talk about prohibition.
4 We use *should* and *shouldn't* **to give advice / talk about obligation and prohibition.**

2 ★ Complete the sentences with *must* or *mustn't* and a verb from the box.

do eat forget ~~keep~~ learn
leave put remember

1 We *must keep* our room tidy.
2 Your brother ___________ his homework while he's watching TV.
3 You ___________ the plates in the dishwasher after dinner.
4 You ___________ your books and papers all over the living room.
5 I ___________ to turn off the oven.
6 Jane ___________ how to cook more than pizza!
7 You ___________ to bring me your dirty clothes.
8 They ___________ all the biscuits. That's too much sugar!

3 ★★ Complete the text with *should* or *shouldn't*.

Feng shui is the old Chinese art of organising your home to bring good health and energy. Here are some ideas about how to improve your house:

- In the bedroom you [1] *should* always clean under the bed so you don't have negative energy. You [2]___________ keep anything there. The bed [3]___________ never be close to the door or under a window.
- In the living room you [4]___________ put a mirror on the wall to give your house more energy, and you [5]___________ have a plant to show love.
- The colour red is good luck, but you [6]___________ have too much of it because it can make people nervous. Finally, you [7]___________ leave space around the things in the house so energy can move around the room.

Do these things and you [8]___________ have any problems!

4 ★★★ Complete the second sentence so it has the same meaning as the first. Use *should, shouldn't, must* or *mustn't*.

1 It's a good idea for them to try feng shui.
They *should try feng shui.*
2 It's not a very good idea to do her homework in the kitchen!
She ___________
3 Our house rule is to wear slippers inside.
You ___________ .
4 My advice is to put your desk under the window.
I think you ___________ .
5 Don't touch that because it's very dangerous!
You ___________ !

5 ★★★ Complete the sentences about your life at home.

1 My parents say I must *be quicker in the bathroom in the morning, because I'm sometimes late for school.*
2 My ___________ says I mustn't ___________
3 I should ___________
____
4 I shouldn't ___________
____

Explore verbs with *up* or *down*

6 ★★ Complete the sentences with the correct form of the verbs in the box and *up* or *down*.

go lie come (x2) put

1 Why did you climb that wall? You should *come down* now.
2 Oh no, it's raining. Can you ___________ the umbrella?
3 We woke up early and watched the sun ___________ .
4 You look tired. Why don't you go and ___________ on your bed?
5 The shops are near here. ___________ to the top of the road and turn left.

Reading

1 ★ Read the texts and match the people with the houses in the pictures.

1 ____________

2 ____________

3 ____________

An unusual place to live

Joey
I live in a windmill! It has five floors and a lot of stairs. The kitchen is at the bottom, the living room is on the first floor, and my bedroom is at the top. It's noisy because of the ***sails*** in the wind, especially in the winter, but the strangest thing is that the rooms are ***round***. Mine is the smallest. It's really difficult to find space for all my things. It's fun here though, and the view is amazing!

Abigail
My friends are always surprised that I live in a 300-year-old house! When my parents bought our house, it was a mess, but now it's beautiful. There are 80 large rooms and 40 bedrooms, so we need a lot of ***furniture*** to ***fill*** it. It's a great place for parties, and playing ***hide and seek***, but it's easy to get lost!

David
My home is a traditional cottage in a country village. I live here with my parents and my two sisters. It's prettier than my friends' houses, but it's very old, so all the rooms are small and uncomfortable, and the ***ceilings*** are low. Also, there's only one bathroom, but my parents love it! My room is in the attic. It's very small, and the floor is not very straight. There's only a bed, a cupboard and a small desk under the window.

2 ★★ Match the words in bold in the text with the definitions.

1 It's a game where some people hide while one person counts to 100. That person then tries to find everyone. *hide and seek*
2 The same shape as a ball or a circle. ____________
3 The part of a room above your head. ____________
4 A windmill usually has four of these and they move in the wind. ____________
5 To make something full or put things in an empty space. ____________
6 Chairs, tables, bed, etc. ____________

3 ★★ Read the text again. Which house is each sentence about? Write *Joey*, *Abigail* or *David*.

1 The house has a lot of different floors. *Joey*
2 It's good for games. ____________
3 It's a strange shape. ____________
4 Visitors can choose a room to sleep in. ____________
5 It's not good for a big family. ____________
6 It isn't quiet. ____________
7 Tall people can't live in a house like this. ____________
8 It wasn't always a nice house. ____________

4 ★★★ Which of these houses would you like to live in? Why? Do you think your family would like it too? Why/Why not? Write at least five sentences.

____
____
____
____
____

Writing

A description of a house

1 Read Corrine's email about an unusual house. Why is she there?

YourMAIL
New
Reply
Delete
Junk
Hi Emma,
How are you? We're staying in a really unusual holiday home for two weeks. It's a tall, old, white lighthouse in Somerset. It's 33 metres high with 120 stairs! There are eight floors with three bedrooms, a living room, a big, modern kitchen and a bathroom. The bedrooms all have small, new showers and the views of the sea are amazing. All the walls are round of course, but the rooms are bigger than you think. The top floor has the big, old light, but it doesn't work now. The lighthouse is 180 years old but everything is modern inside and there's even Wi-Fi. What do you think? Isn't it amazing?!
Love, Corrine

2 Read the email again. What do these numbers mean?

1 120 = *stairs in the lighthouse*
2 8 = ______
3 2 = ______
4 180 = ______
5 33 = ______

Useful language Order of adjectives

3 Read the email again. Write the adjectives.

1 a *tall* ______, ______, ______ lighthouse
2 a ______, ______ kitchen
3 ______, ______ showers
4 the ______, ______ light

4 Put the words in order to make sentences.

1 old / There's / tall / wardrobe / a / white
There's a tall, old, white wardrobe.
2 has got / living room / lamp / small / a / The / yellow / modern
______
3 has got / a / bed / My / old / bedroom / large
______
4 red and blue / The / got / four / big / pillows / bed's / new
______
5 on his desk / a / photo / tiny / black and white / old / There's
______

WRITING TIP

Make it better! ✓✓✓
Use comparatives and superlatives to describe the things in your house.
My sister's bedroom is bigger than mine.

5 Complete the sentences with the comparative or superlative form of the adjectives in brackets.

1 The bathrooms are *smaller than* the bedrooms. (small)
2 My parents have got ______ bedroom in the house. (large)
3 The wardrobe is ______ my bathroom! (big)
4 The furniture in her house is ______ the furniture in my house. (modern)
5 The apartment has got ______ views of the city. (beautiful)

6 Complete the sentences with two or three adjectives to describe the rooms in your house.

1 We've got a *small, new* kitchen.
2 There's a ______ bedroom.
3 There's a ______ living room.
4 I've got a ______ bathroom.

Writing

WRITING TIP

Make it better! ✓ ✓ ✓
Give your opinion of the place, the house or the rooms.
It's a small house, but I really like it because it's warm and comfortable.

7 Which of these sentences does not give an opinion?

1 The house is really unusual.
2 The gardens are really beautiful.
3 There are three large bedrooms.
4 It's really relaxing to walk on the beach near the house.

8 Read Corrine's email again and tick (✓) the information she includes.

a what rooms there are ☐
b the number of bedrooms ☐
c what her favourite room is and why ☐
d what she does in each room ☐
e how old/big the house is ☐
f interesting or unusual features/furniture ☐

PLAN

9 Choose one of these holiday homes to write an email about. Use the information in Exercise 8 and make notes.

a castle in England

a stone cottage in Ireland

a luxury flat in a big city

a houseboat in the Netherlands

WRITE

10 Write the email. Look at page 49 of the Student's Book to help you.

____
____
____
____
____
____
____
____
____
____
____
____

CHECK

11 Check your writing. Can you say YES to these questions?

- Is the information from Exercise 8 in your description?
- Do you use adjectives to describe the room and things in the place?
- Do you use comparative and superlative sentences?
- Do you give your opinion of the place, the rooms or the things?

Do you need to write a second draft?

4 Review

Vocabulary

Things in the home

1 Match the words in the box to the definitions.

sink towel mirror blanket curtains pillow wardrobe ~~carpet~~ shelf cupboard desk

1 This is on the floor. You walk on it. *carpet*
2 You open these in the morning so you can see outside. ____________
3 This is on the bed. It's for your head. ____________
4 This is in the bathroom. You use it after a shower. ____________
5 This is in the bathroom. You can see yourself in it. ____________
6 You put all your clothes in here. ____________
7 You put plates, cups, glasses or food in here. ____________
8 This is on the bed. You use it when it's cold. ____________
9 You put books on this. ____________
10 This is in your bedroom. You do your homework here. ____________
11 This is in the kitchen. You wash dirty plates in here. ____________

Total: 10

Household appliances

2 Complete the sentences with words in the box.

dishwasher ~~washing machine~~ fridge heater lamp cooker hairdryer freezer iron

1 Put the dirty clothes into the *washing machine* .
2 It's cold! Turn on the ____________ .
3 Take some ice out of the ____________ .
4 Put the milk back in the ____________ .
5 I'd like to cook dinner. Turn on the ____________ .
6 Your hair is wet. Go and get the ____________ .
7 Put the dirty plates into the ____________ .
8 Oh no! I burned my shirt with the ____________ !
9 I can't see. It's very dark. Turn on the ____________ .

Total: 8

Language focus

Comparatives

3 Write comparative sentences.

1 London / Edinburgh (big)
London is bigger than Edinburgh.
2 Cheetahs / elephants (fast)
____
3 The Amazon / the Danube (long)
____
4 The Arctic / Iceland (cold)
____
5 Sharks / dolphins (dangerous)
____
6 Hawaii / Alaska (warm)
____
7 Hotels / youth hostels (expensive)
____

Total: 6

Superlatives

4 Write sentences in the superlative.

1 Russia / big / country / in the world
Russia is the biggest country in the world.
2 The cheetah / fast / animal in the world
____
3 The *Mona Lisa* / famous / painting in the world
____
4 The University of Al-Karaouine in Morocco / old / university in the world
____
5 The Himalayas / high / mountains in the world
____
6 The Australian box jellyfish / poisonous / creature in the world
____

Total: 5

must/mustn't, should/shouldn't

5 Complete the sentences with *must*, *mustn't*, *should* or *shouldn't* and the verb.

1 It's a good idea to get up early.
You *should get* up early.

2 It isn't ok to talk in the library.
You ___ quiet in the library.

3 It is against the rules to eat sandwiches in the classroom.
We ___ sandwiches in the classroom.

4 It isn't a good idea to talk and eat at the same time.
You ___ ___ at the same time.

5 You can't use your mobile during a test.
You ___ your mobile during a test.

Total: 4

Language builder

6 Complete the conversation with the missing words. Circle the correct options.

Dear Becky,
We [1]___ a wonderful time on our holiday in Australia. We [2]___ at a beautiful beach hotel. It's [3]___ than at home! I love [4]___ in the ocean. We [5]___ snorkelling near the beach yesterday when we saw [6]___ dolphins! I think they're [7]___ sea creatures in the world! I took [8]___ of pictures!
I [9]___ remember to send you some photos. It's really important to be careful in the sun over here. They told us we [10]___ wear hats all the time and we [11]___ out in the middle of the day.
See you soon!
Angie

	a	b	c
1	have	(b) 're having	do have
2	stay	're staying	stayed
3	sunny	sunniest	sunnier
4	swim	swimming	swam
5	was	were	are
6	much	any	some
7	the beautiful	the most beautiful	the more beautiful
8	a lot	some	many
9	must	mustn't	should
10	should	aren't	mustn't
11	aren't going	must go	shouldn't go

Total: 10

Vocabulary builder

7 Choose the correct word.

1 My uncle's daughter is my *cousin* .
a aunt b cousin c mother

2 We studied the rivers of France in ___ today.
a Geography b History c Maths

3 Your bedroom is really ___ . Pick up all those things!
a unfriendly b unfair c untidy

4 He ran very fast but he couldn't ___ them.
a climb b chase c catch

5 Is there any ice cream in the ___ ?
a cooker b freezer c fridge

6 He plays the piano and the guitar. He's an amazing ___ .
a dancer b scientist c musician

7 I think there are some biscuits in the ___ .
a cupboard b wardrobe c sink

8 Where's the ___ ? I'm going to lie down on the sofa.
a carpet b blanket c towel

9 We're ___ in the park at the moment. Do you want to come?
a walk b walking c doing

10 When the sun ___ we were all sleeping in our beds.
a put up b went up c came up

Total: 9

Speaking

8 Circle the correct options.

Mum: Tom, [1]**(can) / shall** you help me in the kitchen?
Tom: OK. [2]**Do / Shall** I make the salad?
Mum: Yes, please, and [3]**can / shall** you do me a favour and take the dog out for a walk after dinner?
Tom: Sorry, I [4]**can't / don't**. I need to finish my homework. [5]**I'll / I** ask Sue.
Mum: That's OK. [6]**I'll / Shall I** do it.
Tom: [7]**Shall / Could** I tell Sue and Dad it's time for dinner?
Mum: Yes, please.

Total: 6

Total: 58

Get it right! Unit 4

Comparatives and superlatives

Remember that:
- with short adjectives we add ***-er*** or ***-est***.
- with long adjectives we use ***more*** or ***the most***.

1 Find and correct five more mistakes with comparatives and superlatives.

Louisa: What do you think of my new bedroom? It's ~~more bigger~~ *bigger* than my old room.
Izzie: It's great! I love the big windows. It's more lighter than your old room too.
Louisa: Yes. And I've got some new furniture. Do you like it?
Izzie: Yes, it's moderner, isn't it? The old stuff was … well, more traditional.
Louisa: I know, it was awful! I had the most old wardrobe in the world!
Izzie: This one's much more nicer. You've got loads of space for all your clothes.
Louisa: And come look at the view from the window. It's the beautifullest view in town.

must/mustn't, should/shouldn't

Remember, we use the infinitive without ***to*** after ***should*** and ***must***.

✓ *You **should avoid** watching TV.*
✗ ~~*You should to avoid watching TV.*~~
✓ *You **mustn't eat** a big meal before going to bed.*
✗ ~~*You mustn't eating a big meal before going to bed.*~~

2 Are the sentences correct? Correct the incorrect sentences.

Six tips for exam success

1. You should ~~to~~ make a timetable of all the work you need to do.
2. You must getting at least 8 hours of sleep every night.
3. You shouldn't work late in the evening.
4. You must to remember to take a break.
5. You should going for a walk every day.
6. You mustn't forget to eat!
7. You should to drink a lot of water.

Prepositions of place

Remember that:
- we use ***in*** with rooms, towns and countries.
  ✓ *Maisie lives **in** the USA.*
- we use ***on*** with surfaces, e.g. *floor, wall, table.*
  ✓ *There is a computer **on** my desk.*
- we usually use ***at*** with buildings, e.g. *school, home.*
  ✓ *We stayed **at** a very unusual hotel.*

3 Complete the sentences with *at, in* or *on*.

1. *In* the kitchen, there's a fridge, a cooker and a dishwasher.
2. There is a library at school, but I prefer to do my homework ______ home.
3. I like the picture ______ the wall in the bedroom.
4. When it's cold, I put a blanket ______ the bed.
5. There's a lamp ______ the table in the living room.
6. I bought a beautiful mirror ______ San Francisco.

Spell it right! Comparative adjectives

Remember that:
- with short adjectives (one syllable) ending in vowel + consonant, we double the final consonant and add ***-er*** to form the comparative.
  His bedroom is big. → *His bedroom is **bigger** than mine.*
- we do not use ***more*** or ***very*** before comparative adjectives ending in ***-er***.
  ✓ *His bedroom is **bigger** than mine.*
  ✗ ~~*His bedroom is more bigger than mine.*~~
  ✗ ~~*His bedroom is very bigger than mine.*~~
- with long adjectives (two syllables +) we use ***more*** before the adjective.
  Their house is beautiful. → *Their house is **more** beautiful than ours.*
- with adjectives that have two syllables and end in *-y*, we remove the *-y* and add ***-ier***.
  Your garden is pretty. → *Your garden is **prettier** than ours.*

4 Write the comparative forms of the adjectives.

1. cold *colder*
2. expensive ______
3. tidy ______
4. comfortable ______
5. small ______
6. relaxing ______
7. high ______
8. easy ______

Speaking extra

Shopping

1 ★ **Put the words in order to make questions and answers from the Real talk video in the Student's Book.**

1 do / money / How / you / your / spend / ?

____

2 my / spend / food / I / money / usually / on

____

3 love / friends / shopping / going / with / my / I

____

4 friends / my / to / go / money / with / I / out / use

____

5 spend / a / tickets / lot / of / on / I / concert / money

____

2 ★★ 09 **Listen and choose the correct answer.**

Conversation 1:

1 The girl wants to buy **a sweater** / **trainers**.

Conversation 2:

2 The boy wants to buy a **medium** / **large** T-shirt.

3 He prefers the **red** / **black** one.

Conversation 3:

4 The girl wants to buy **jeans** / **a shirt**.

5 She doesn't like the **size** / **colour**.

3 ★ **Read the conversation. Which game does Oliver buy?**

Oliver:	Excuse me, I'd [1]__________ to buy the new *MegaZoo 5* video game.
Shop assistant:	Sure, it's over there.
Oliver:	How [2]__________ is it?
Shop assistant:	It's £26.99.
Oliver:	And how much is the *Doghouse* game?
Shop assistant:	It's £45.99.
Oliver:	OK, I think I'd [3]__________ *MegaZoo 5*, then. Can I [4]__________ the game first?
Shop assistant:	Yes, it's in this machine here.
Oliver:	Thanks.
Shop assistant:	[5]__________ is it?
Oliver:	It's great! I'll [6]__________ it.

4 ★★ 10 **Complete the conversation in Exercise 3 with the words in the box. Then listen and check.**

prefer	play	take	much	like	How

Focus on pronunciation

5 ★ 11 **How do you say these prices? Listen and repeat.**

1 £1.99
2 £15
3 £180
4 £56.99
5 £10.50

6 ★ 12 **Listen to the conversation. What colour boots does Emily buy?**

Emily:	Excuse me, [1]__________ to a buy some boots.
Shop assistant:	Sure. What about these, or those ones over there?
Emily:	I think [2]__________ them in black.
Shop assistant:	OK, over here. Do you like these?
Emily:	Yes, they're quite cool. [3]__________ are they?
Shop assistant:	They're £65.99.
Emily:	[4]__________ them on?
Shop assistant:	Of course. [5]__________ are you?
Emily:	I'm usually a size 7.
Shop assistant:	Here you are. How are they?
Emily:	I like them but have you got anything cheaper?
Shop assistant:	What about these? They're almost the same but they're £45.75 and they're brown.
Emily:	Yes, they're great! I'll [6]__________ them.

7 ★★★ 12 **Listen again and complete the conversation.**

8 ★★ 12 **Listen again and check your answers. Then listen and repeat the conversation.**

Speaking extra

Speculating

1 ★ **Join the parts of the sentences from the Real talk video in the Student's Book.**

1 He can run faster
2 She's 20
3 She also helps
4 His family was very poor
5 He saved his little sister

a a lot of children's charities.
b and she's an amazing dancer.
c but he worked hard and went to college.
d from a burning house.
e than anyone on the planet.

2 ★★ 13 **Listen and choose the correct answer.**

Conversation 1:
1 The boy and girl see **someone famous** / **a famous photographer**.
Conversation 2:
2 The boy and girl are at a **museum** / **bookshop**.
3 They **agree** / **don't agree** on what the picture is.
Conversation 3:
4 They are in a **History** / **Art** class.

3 ★ **Read the conversation. Match the jobs with the people in the photos.**

dancer ___	scientist ___
musician ___	firefighter ___

a 
b 
c 
d 

Boy: So what do we have to do?
Girl: You never listen, do you? We have to look at these photos and decide what jobs they do.
Boy: Just by looking at the photos.
Girl: Yes. So what do you [1]___________ he is?
Boy: Well, he [2]___________ very strong … and brave, I think. So a firefighter, something like that.
Girl: Yeah, I agree. This guy looks very serious but he's got a friendly face. He [3]___________ be an artist.
Boy: Yes, but look at the way he's standing. I [4]___________ he's a dancer.
Girl: Oh yeah. You're right. What about this woman?
Boy: I'm not [5]___________ .
Girl: Well, she's wearing a white coat so could be either a scientist or a nurse.
Boy: That's [6]___________ .
Girl: She [7]___________ works in a laboratory so she's a scientist.
Boy: Right. What about this woman?
Girl: I reckon she's a musician.
Boy: OK, write it down. Come on, let's check our answers.

4 ★★ 14 **Complete the conversation in Exercise 3 with the words in the box. Then listen and check.**

reckon	possible	looks	think
definitely	could	sure	

Focus on pronunciation

5 ★ 15 **Listen to the sentences. Do they go up or down? Listen and repeat.**

1 I'm not sure.
2 That's possible.
3 She could be a vet.
4 I reckon she's an artist.

6 ★ 16 **Listen to the conversation. Whose phone is it?**

Mark: Look! A mobile phone.
Olivia: Oh yeah, whose [1]___________ ?
Mark: I'm [2]___________ . It's [3]___________ someone from our class because it's in our classroom.
Olivia: [4]___________ very new. Do you think it's the teacher's phone?
Mark: [5]___________ . [6]___________ it's a student's phone. Look at the photo here.
Olivia: Oh yeah. She's definitely not in our class.
Mark: [7]___________ someone's sister or cousin.
Olivia: You're right. Hold on. [8]___________ it's Vanessa's – I've seen Vanessa with that dress on so that could be her sister.
Mark: Right, let's go and find her.

7 ★★★ 16 **Listen again and complete the conversation.**

Speaking extra

Telling someone your news

1 ★ **Complete the sentences from the Real talk video in the Student's Book with the words in the box.**

the lock	the winning goal	a new shirt	my cat

1 A couple of weeks ago ___________ Jasper escaped.
2 The bike was still there but ___________ wasn't.
3 I scored ___________ in the last five minutes of the game.
4 Last weekend I wore ___________ to my friend's birthday party and she was wearing the same one.

2 ★★ 17 **Listen and write the answers.**

Conversation 1:
1 What month is it?
____

Conversation 2:
2 What was the boy doing?
____
3 What kind of animal flew into the window?
____

Conversation 3:
4 What are they talking about?
____

3 ★ **Read the conversation. What did Andy find in the park?**

Andy: Did you hear about this morning?
Louise: No, what?
Andy: Something [1]___________ happened while we were walking to school. We heard a baby crying in the park. But we couldn't see anyone.
Louise: So [2]___________ did you do?
Andy: We started looking for it – the sound got louder and louder. It was coming from a park bench.
Louise: So did you find it?
Andy: No, because it wasn't a baby! It was a mobile phone! I answered it and a man started shouting at me!
Louise: What did you [3]___________ ?
Andy: At first, I didn't know what to say and then, I said, 'I'm sorry. You've got the wrong number.'
Louise: What happened [4]___________ ?
Andy: Another man ran up to us and said it was his phone, so we gave it to him. He said something about his boss being really angry. And then he ran off again.
Louise: How [5]___________ !

4 ★★ 18 **Complete the conversation in Exercise 3 with the words in the box. Then listen and check your answers.**

next	what	unusual	do	weird

Focus on pronunciation

5 ★ 19 **Listen to the words and phrases. Do they go up or down? Listen and repeat.**

1 Really?
2 What?
3 How weird!
4 I know!
5 Cool!

6 ★ 20 **Listen to the conversation. Who were the photographers waiting for?**

Ben: [1]___________ happened yesterday.
Peter: What?
Ben: I was walking out of the school and I saw lots of photographers waiting at the door.
Peter: [2]___________ .
Ben: I know. I didn't understand what they were doing there.
Peter: So [3]___________ ?
Ben: Well, I waited on the other side of the street. Then Mrs Carter, our History teacher, came out. And all the photographers started taking photos of her.
Peter: Really? Your History teacher? [4]___________ ?
Ben: Well, they started asking her questions about money.
Peter: Money? And [5]___________ ?
Ben: She said she was really happy.

7 ★★★ 20 **Listen again and complete the conversation.**

8 ★★ 20 **Listen again and check your answers. Then listen and repeat the conversation.**

9 ★ 21 **Listen to the end of the conversation. What happened?**

Speaking extra

Asking for and offering help

1 ★ **Complete the sentences from the Real talk video in the Student's Book with the words in the box.**

garden	quieter	expensive	space	rooms	light

1 They're usually bigger so there's more ___________ .
2 I think houses because they can be ___________ .
3 Flats are small and they sometimes don't get much ___________ .
4 It has a lot of ___________ and it's really comfortable.
5 There isn't usually a ___________ with a flat.
6 Houses near the centre of big cities are really ___________ .

2 ★★ 22 **Listen and answer the questions.**

Conversation 1:
1 How does the boy help the woman?
____

Conversation 2:
2 What did Sarah leave at school?
____
3 Where will Helen go later?
____

Conversation 3:
4 What does the boy have to do?
____
5 What does the girl want?
____

3 ★ **Read the conversation. What do Connor and Jonas put in the wardrobe?**

Connor: My mum says I should tidy my room before I go out.
Jonas: Well, she's right. I'll [1]___________ you a hand.
Connor: OK, let's see. The books shouldn't be on the floor. I should put them all up on that shelf.
Jonas: Here, [2]___________ do that. Oh look, *The Lord of the Rings*. Did you like it?
Connor: Yes, it's really good. Can you [3]___________ me a favour?
Jonas: Yes, of [4]___________ .
Connor: Can you give me a [5]___________ and put this blanket in the wardrobe?
Jonas: [6]___________ I put this pillow in there as well?
Connor: Yes, please!

4 ★★ 23 **Complete the conversation in Exercise 3 with the words in the box. Then listen and check.**

do	I'll	give	Shall	course	hand

Focus on pronunciation

5 ★ 24 **Listen to the questions. Do they go up or down? Listen and repeat.**

1 Can you give me a hand?
2 Can you put this on the shelf?
3 Can you do me a favour?
4 Can you help me with this?

6 ★ 25 **Listen to the conversation. What do Nick and Lisa put in the freezer?**

Nick: Come on, the computer's ready. Let's play.
Lisa: Hang on. I can't. My dad did the shopping and he wants me to put it all away.
Nick: OK, I'll give you [1]___________ .
Lisa: Great. That way we'll finish sooner.
Nick: [2]___________ put the milk and cheese in the fridge?
Lisa: Yes, please!
Nick: Anything else?
Lisa: We should put the ice cream and the pizzas in the freezer.
Nick: [3]___________ !
Lisa: And I need to wash all this fruit. [4]___________ me a hand?
Nick: Sure: Put it all in the sink and [5]___________ .
Lisa: Oh and another thing. Can you do me [6]___________ ?
Nick: Sure.
Lisa: Can you start making lunch? I'm hungry!
Nick: Ha ha ha! Come on. Mario is waiting!

7 ★★★ 25 **Listen again and complete the conversation.**

8 ★★ 25 **Listen again and check your answers. Then listen and repeat the conversation.**

Language focus extra

UNIT S

Subject pronouns and *be*

1 Complete the questions with *am, is* or *are*. Then match the question with the answer.

1 When *is* your birthday? *c*
2 ______ your friends at home? ______
3 How old ______ your aunt? ______
4 What time ______ it? ______
5 ______ you from Chile? ______

a No, they aren't.
b It's 10 o'clock.
c It's on 2 June.
d No, I'm not.
e She's 48.

Possessive *'s*

2 Add *'s* or *'* to the correct place in the sentences.

1 Martin*'s* pencil case is black and white.
2 My best friend bike is in the sports hall.
3 My parents names are Cristina and Robbie.
4 My cousin friends are in my class.
5 My three friends books are on the floor.

there is/are + some and *any*

3 Match the sentence halves.

1 There isn't *c*
2 Are there ______
3 There aren't ______
4 There's ______
5 Is there ______

a any orange juice in that bag?
b some water in the canteen.
c any milk on the table.
d any computers in your school library?
e any dictionaries in our classroom.

Have got + a/an

4 Read about Rachel, Ben and Tom's things and complete the table with answers about you. Use the information to write Yes/No questions with *have* and short answers.

	Rachel	Ben and Tom	You
a dog or a cat	✓	✗	______
a laptop	✗	✓	______

1 *Has Rachel got a dog or a cat?* *Yes, she has.*
2 *Has Rachel got a laptop?* ______
3 ______ ? ______
4 ______ ? ______
5 ______ ? ______
6 ______ ? ______

Present simple: affirmative and negative

5 Write sentences with the correct form of the present simple.

1 I / not ride / my bike to school
I don't ride my bike to school.
2 My friends / play / basketball in the school team
______
3 My teacher / go / swimming in the sea every day
______
4 We / not have / lunch at home
______
5 My dad / not work / near here
______

Present simple: questions

6 Put the words in order to make questions and write the answers.

1 you / Where / do / live / ?
Where do you live? I live near my school.
2 you and your friends / snowboarding / Do / go / ?
______
3 lunch / What time / you / have / do / ?
______
4 Does / mum / skiing / go / your / ?
______
5 dinner / dad / Does / TV / after / your / watch / ?
______

Adverbs of frequency

7 Circle the correct words.

1 I **often play** / **play often** volleyball in the summer.
2 My sister and I **do usually** / **usually do** our homework in our bedroom.
3 I **am sometimes** / **sometimes am** tired on Monday morning.
4 We **sometimes go** / **go sometimes** surfing.
5 It **is never** / **never is** hot in December.

Language focus extra

Present continuous: affirmative and negative

1 Complete the sentences with the present continuous form of the verb in brackets.

1 Lots of people *are shopping* in the mall today. (shop)
2 I ________ for a new dress. (look)
3 My mum ________ a magazine in the cafe. (read)
4 She ________ coffee. (not drink)
5 My brother ________ a computer game. (play)
6 We ________ a lot of money. (not spend)

Present continuous: *Wh-* questions

2 Write questions using the present continuous.

1 What / you / buy
What are you buying ?
2 Where / they / go
________ ?
3 Who / she / meet
________ ?
4 What / Jenny / watch
________ ?
5 Why / we / wait
________ ?
6 What / Joe / wear
________ ?

Present continuous: *Yes/No* questions

3 Read what Maria, Judy and Tim are doing and complete the table with answers about you. Use the information to write *Yes/No* questions and short answers in the present continuous.

	Maria	Judy and Tim	You
visit the mall	✗	✓	________
study grammar	✓	✗	________

1 *Is Maria visiting the mall* ? *No* , *she isn't* .
2 ________ ? ____ , ________ .
3 ________ ? ____ , ________ .
4 ________ ? ____ , ________ .
5 ________ ? ____ , ________ .
6 ________ ? ____ , ________ .

Spelling: *-ing* form

4 Complete the chart with the *-ing* form of the verbs in the box.

~~do~~ get look make run write

Add *-ing*	Remove the *-e* and add *-ing*	Double consonant and add *-ing*
1 *doing*	3 ________	5 ________
2 ________	4 ________	6 ________

Present simple vs. continuous

5 Complete the sentences with the present simple or present continuous form of the verbs in the box.

buy not do ~~eat~~ not talk visit

1 We *are eating* pizza right now.
2 I ________ my homework at the moment.
3 They often ________ the mall on Saturdays.
4 My mum ________ books in that shop.
5 Joe ________ on his mobile right now.

(don't) want to, would(n't) like to, would prefer to

6 Circle the correct options.

1 I don't **want** / **like** to go to school today.
2 Jack likes playing football but he'd **want** / **prefer** to go swimming today.
3 Would you **want** / **like** to come with me?
4 I wouldn't **like** / **prefer** to do judo.
5 We've got Maths and English homework today. I'd **want** / **prefer** to do English first.

(not) enough + noun

7 Complete the sentences with *enough* and the words in the box.

money milk ~~paper~~ chairs time

1 There isn't *enough* *paper* for everyone.
2 I'd like to buy a skateboard but I haven't got ________ ________ .
3 Sit down, everybody. Oh sorry, we haven't got ________ ________ .
4 We can't go to the bookshop now. We haven't got ________ ________ . It's late.
5 Have you got ________ ________ for three glasses?

Language focus extra

was/were: affirmative and negative

1 Complete the sentences with the correct form of *was* or *were*.

At school, I [1] *wasn't* (not) very good at sport but I [2] ______ good at dancing. My friends [3] ______ all crazy about football. They [4] ______ (not) interested in dancing. I saw my first ballet when I [5] ______ 12 years old. It [6] ______ amazing!

Past simple: affirmative and negative

2 Write sentences in the past simple.

1 Tim / play / football / yesterday
Tim played football yesterday.
2 Joanna / go skiing / last winter
______
3 Gina and Tony / grow up / in Canada
______
4 We / not want / to practise the piano / last weekend
______
5 I / not play / tennis / at school / when I was little
______
6 Nicky / not win / the singing competition / last week
______

Past simple: irregular verbs

3 Write the past simple of each verb.

1 have *had*
2 make ______
3 become ______
4 write ______
5 get ______
6 see ______

Past simple: spelling

4 Complete the chart with the past simple form of each verb.

like stop dance study try ~~wait~~

Add *-ed*	Add *-d*
1 *waited*	2 ______ 3 ______

Remove the last letter and add *-ied*	Double the last consonant and add *-ed*
4 ______ 5 ______	6 ______

was/were: questions

5 Complete the questions with the past simple of *be* and write the short answers.

1 *Were* you in judo class yesterday?
Yes, I was . ✓
2 ______ Jake good at sports at school?
______ . ✓
3 ______ they in the supermarket this morning? No, ______ . ✗
4 ______ he unfriendly at the party?
______ . ✗
5 ______ your cousin Julia in Paris last year?
______ . ✓
6 ______ the police officers at your school yesterday? ______ . ✓

Past simple: *Wh-* questions

6 Write a question for each answer. Use the past simple.

1 What *did you drink* ?
I drank some lemonade.
2 Where ______ ?
He went to a concert.
3 When ______ ?
They started school at 9 am.
4 Who ______ ?
She met her sister.
5 What ______ ?
We ate some sandwiches.
6 Why ______ ?
We stayed at home because it was raining.

Past simple: *Yes/No* questions

7 Read what Helen, Sam and Abby did last weekend and complete the table with answers about you. Use the information to write *Yes/No* questions and short answers in the past simple.

	Helen	Sam and Abby	You
eat pizza	✗	✓	______
go shopping	✓	✗	______

1 *Did Helen eat pizza* ? *No* , *she didn't* .
2 ______ ? ______ , ______ .
3 ______ ? ______ , ______ .
4 ______ ? ______ , ______ .
5 ______ ? ______ , ______ .
6 ______ ? ______ , ______ .

Language focus extra

Past continuous: affirmative

1 Complete the sentences with the past continuous forms of the verbs in the box.

cook chase drink ~~read~~ steal talk buy watch

At 3 pm yesterday afternoon …

1 …Peter *was reading* a book.
2 …Julie ________ on the phone.
3 …Jason and Angie ________ dinner.
4 …we ________ TV.
5 …I ________ a cup of tea.
6 … the burglars ________ the money.
7 … my parents ________ a new car.
8 … the dog ________ the cat around the house.

Past continuous: negative

2 Complete the sentences with the negative form of the past continuous. Use contractions.

1 Peter *wasn't playing* football. (play)
2 Julie ________ emails. (write)
3 Jason and Angie ________ in the garden. (sit)
4 We ________ our bikes. (ride)
5 I ________ a sandwich. (eat)
6 The burglars ________ any noise. (make)
7 My parents ________ to the shop. (walk)
8 The dog ________ in the park. (run)

Past continuous: *Wh-* questions

3 Write *Wh-* questions with the past continuous.

1 What *were you doing* ? (you / do)
2 Where ________ ? (they / go)
3 Who ________ ? (she / talk to)
4 Why ________ ? (he / leave)
5 Where ________ ? (Jacky / sit)
6 What ________ ? (your friends / watch)
7 Why ________ ? (they / go)
8 Who ________ ? (she / meet)

Past continuous: *Yes/No* questions

4 Read what Jessica, Luke and Nina were doing at 5 pm yesterday and complete the table with answers about you. Then use the information to write *Yes/No* questions and short answers with the past continuous.

	Jessica	Luke and Nina	You
watch TV	✗	✓	________
do homework	✓	✗	________

1 *Was Jessica watching TV* ? *No* , *she wasn't* .
2 ________ ? ____ , ________ .
3 ________ ? ____ , ________ .
4 ________ ? ____ , ________ .
5 ________ ? ____ , ________ .
6 ________ ? ____ , ________ .

Past simple vs. continuous

5 Complete the sentences with the past simple or the past continuous.

1 I *was reading* (read) in bed when I ________ (hear) a loud noise in the street.
2 No one ________ (watch) when the burglars ________ (break) into the bank.
3 The money ________ (disappear) while the guards ________ (have) lunch.
4 While we ________ (watch) TV, the alarm ________ (go) off.
5 When we ________ (look) out of the window, police officers ________ (enter) the bank.
6 The burglars ________ (count) their money when the police ________ (catch) them.

could(n't)

6 Complete the sentences with *could/couldn't* and the words in brackets.

1 I *could speak* French when I was five. (speak)
2 She ________ because she was afraid of water. (not swim)
3 Sam ________ the top shelf because he was too short. (not reach)
4 ________ the piano when he was small? (Tony, play)
5 We ________ because he spoke very quietly. (not hear)
6 ________ a bike when you were a child? (you, ride)

Language focus extra

Comparatives

1 Complete the table with the comparative forms of the words in the box.

~~comfortable~~ expensive nice
interesting safe tall

Add *-r* or *-er*	*more* + adjective
___________	*more comfortable*
___________	___________
___________	___________

2 Complete the sentences with the comparative form of the words in brackets.

1 My house is *smaller than* your house. (small)
2 Jack's room is ___________ Katrina's room. (tidy)
3 Laura's homework is ___________ Abby's homework. (good)
4 This new hotel is ___________ the old hotel. (comfortable)
5 The sofa is ___________ the armchair. (expensive)

Superlatives

3 Write superlative sentences with the words below.

1 The New South China Mall / large / shopping centre / world
The New South China Mall is the largest shopping centre in the world.
2 Vostok in Antarctica / cold / place on Earth
____
3 My bedroom / good / room in the house
____
4 This is / comfortable / chair
____
5 I'm not / bad / student / in our class
____

Comparatives and superlatives

4 Circle the correct form.

1 **A:** I think New York is **more exciting / the most exciting** city in the world!
B: I don't agree. I think that London is **more exciting / the most exciting** than New York.
2 **A:** Buses are **safer / the safest** than trains.
B: I don't agree. I think that trains are **safer / the safest** form of transport.
3 **A:** I think that Tokyo is **more expensive / the most expensive** city in the world.
B: I read that Singapore is **more expensive / the most expensive** than Tokyo.

must/mustn't

5 Complete the sentences with *must* or *mustn't* and the verb in brackets.

1 You *mustn't talk* during the lesson. (talk)
2 You ___________ your homework on time. (do)
3 You ___________ sandwiches in the classroom. (eat)
4 You ___________ your friend's homework. (copy)
5 You ___________ on the chairs. (stand)
6 You ___________ carefully to the teacher. (listen)

should/shouldn't

6 Complete the sentences with *should* or *shouldn't* and the verbs in the box.

take go meet phone stay ~~wear~~

1 It's cold today. You *should wear* a warm coat.
2 The train leaves at 10 am. We ___________ at 9.45.
3 It's raining. You ___________ your umbrella.
4 It's late. You ___________ to bed now.
5 I've got an exam tomorrow. I ___________ up late.
6 You've got a toothache. You ___________ the dentist.

should/shouldn't: questions

7 Put the words in the correct order to make questions. Then complete the answers.

1 we / Should / get up / tomorrow / early
A: *Should we get up early tomorrow* ?
B: Yes, *we should* .
2 wear / I / to the party / should / What
A: ___________ ?
B: You ___________ your blue dress.
3 use / my calculator / in the exam / Should / I
A: ___________ ?
B: No, ___________
4 we / When / meet / should
A: ___________ ?
B: We ___________ at 9 am.
5 Should / book / I / a hotel
A: ___________ ?
B: Yes, ___________
6 What / do / should / this afternoon / I
A: ___________ ?
B: You ___________ your homework.

Irregular verbs

infinitive	past simple	past participle
be	was/were	been
become	became	become
begin	began	begun
break	broke	broken
build	built	built
buy	bought	bought
catch	caught	caught
choose	chose	chosen
come	came	come
do	did	done
drink	drank	drunk
drive	drove	driven
eat	ate	eaten
fall	fell	fallen
feed	fed	fed
feel	felt	felt
find	found	found
fly	flew	flown
get	got	got
give	gave	given
go	went	gone
have	had	had
hear	heard	heard
keep	kept	kept
know	knew	known
learn	learnt/learned	learnt/learned
leave	left	left
lose	lost	lost
make	made	made
meet	met	met
pay	paid	paid
put	put	put
read	read	read
run	ran	run
say	said	said
see	saw	seen
send	sent	sent
sit	sat	sat
sleep	slept	slept
speak	spoke	spoken
spend	spent	spent
swim	swam	swum
take	took	taken
teach	taught	taught
tell	told	told
think	thought	thought
wear	wore	worn
win	won	won
write	wrote	written

Phonemic script

consonants	
/p/	pencil
/b/	bag
/t/	town
/d/	day
/ʧ/	cheese
/ʤ/	juice
/k/	cake
/g/	get
/f/	food
/v/	very
/θ/	Thursday
/ð/	that
/s/	speak
/z/	zebra
/ʃ/	shoe
/ʒ/	usually
/m/	mum
/n/	name
/ŋ/	sing
/h/	house
/l/	like
/r/	red
/w/	water
/j/	you

vowels	
/iː/	see
/ɪ/	sit
/ʊ /	book
/uː/	zoo
/e /	pen
/ə/	teacher
/ɜː/	bird
/ɔː/	boring
/æ/	that
/ʌ/	run
/ɑː/	car
/ɒ/	lost

diphthongs	
/eɪ/	say
/ɪə/	hear
/ʊə/	pure
/ɔɪ/	enjoy
/əʊ/	know
/eə/	chair
/aɪ/	buy
/aʊ/	now

Thanks and acknowledgments

The authors and publishers would like to thank a number of people whose support has proved invaluable during the planning, writing and production process of this course.

We would like to thank Diane Nicholls for researching and writing the Get it Right pages.

We would like to thank the following for their contributions: Emma Heyderman for writing the Language focus extra starter page and Andrew Jurascheck and Ruth Cox for editorial work.

We would also like to thank the teams of educational consultants, representatives and managers working for Cambridge University Press in various countries around the world.

The authors and publishers are grateful to the following contributors:

Blooberry: concept design
emc design limited: text design and layouts
QBS Learning: photo selection
emc design limited: cover design
David Morritt and Ian Harker - DSound: audio recordings

Development of this publication has made use of the Cambridge English Corpus (CEC). The CEC is a computer database of contemporary spoken and written English, which currently stands at over one billion words. It includes British English, American English and other varieties of English. It also includes the Cambridge Learner Corpus, developed in collaboration with the University of Cambridge ESOL Examinations. Cambridge University Press has built up the CEC to provide evidence about language use that helps to produce better language teaching materials.

The publishers are grateful to the following for permission to reproduce copyright photographs and material:

p. 3 (BR): Alamy/©Stockbroker/MBI; p. 6 (BL): Shutterstock Images/Jacek Chabraszewski; p. 7 (CR): Alamy/©Ian Pilbeam; p. 8 (TR): Alamy/©Tetra Images; p. 9 (TR): Corbis/Image Source; p. 10 (B): Alamy/©Jose Luis Pelaez Inc/Blend Images; p. 11 (T): AP Images/Paul Brown/Rex Features; p. 12 (L): Shutterstock Images/discpicture; p. 12 (TR): ©David L. Moore – Lifestyle; p. 19 (BR): Shutterstock Images/Bryan Busovicki; p. 21 (TC): REX/Ken McKay; p. 21 (1): REX/Steve Meddle; p. 21 (2): REX/Ken McKay/Thames; p. 21 (3): Alamy/©Mar Photographics; p. 22 (TL): Alamy/©Ian Shaw; p. 29 (BR): Alamy/©Catchlight Visual Services; p. 31 (T): Newscom/Quique Curbelow/Epa; p. 32 (T): AP Images/Steven Senne; p. 37 (1): Shutterstock Images/Winston Link; p. 37 (2): Shutterstock Images/fokusgood; p. 37 (3): Alamy/©Martin Wierink; p. 37(4): Margo Harrison/Shutterstock; p. 37 (5): Alamy/©DJC; p. 37 (6): Shutterstock Images/Baloncici; p. 37 (7): Shutterstock Images/Elena Elisseeva; p. 37 (8): Shutterstock Images/ Venus Angel; p. 37 (9): Shutterstock Images/Sergey Karpov; p. 37 (10): Alamy/©Tyson Ellis/Built Images; p. 37 (11): Shutterstock Images/Simon Bratt; p. 38 (TR): Getty/Bloomberg; p. 39 (2): Shutterstock Images/ Africa Studio; p. 39 (3): Shutterstock Images/Photoseeker; p. 39 (7): Shutterstock Images/Maxal Tamor; p. 39 (8): Shutterstock Images/Mats; p. 41 (TL): Shutterstock Images/Lilly Trott; p. 41 (CL): Alamy/©Tim Gainey; p. 41 (BL): Alamy/©Adams Picture Library t/a apl; p. 42 (L): Getty/Anthony Collins; p. 43 (TR): Alamy/©Image Source; p. 43 (CR): Alamy/©Ian Dagnall; p. 43 (CL): Alamy/©Imagestate Media Partners Limited - Impact Photos; p. 43 (BL): Shutterstock Images/Kwiatek7;vp. 47 (7): Alamy/©Henry George Beeker; p. 47 (8): Shutterstock Images/ windu; p. 47 (9): Alamy/©acek Lasa;vp. 49 (CR): Alamy/©Dream Pictures/ Blend Images; p. 51 (CL): Alamy/©Jim West; p. 51 (BL): Alamy/©Caryn Becker; p. 55 (TL): Corbis/Marc Romanelli/Blend Images; p. 57 (1): Rex features/Theo Kingma; p. 57 (2): Rex features/Theo Kingma; p. 57 (3): Rex features/Everett Collection; p. 57 (4): Rex features/Masatoshi Okauchi; p. 59 (TR): Superstock/ Minden Pictures; p. 59 (CR): Alamy/©dpa picture alliance archive; p. 60 (T): Alamy/©Mark Thomas; p. 61 (TR): Alamy/©Beyond Fotomedia GmbH; p. 61 (CL): Shutterstock Images/ Irina Schmidt; p. 62 (T): Corbis/Nancy Ney; p. 68 (TL): Superstock/ ChameleonsEye; p. 68 (TR): Corbis/Superstock; p. 68 (BL): Alamy/©Paul Carstairs; p. 68 (BR): Alamy/©Colin Hawkins/Cultura Creative; p. 69 (1): Alamy/©ROYER Philippe/SAGAPHOTO.COM; p. 69 (2): Getty/Mike Harrington; p. 69 (3): Shutterstock Images/Vitalii Nesterchuk; p. 69 (4): Shutterstock Images/abaghda; p. 71 (C): Superstock/Minden Pictures; p. 71 (BL): Superstock/Minden Pictures; p. 71 (BC): Alamy/©John Warburton-Lee Photography; p. 72 (TL): Alamy/©PHOVOIR; p. 73 (TL): Shutterstock Images/kearia; p. 73 (BC): Shutterstock Images/TanjaJovicic; p. 73 (TR): Shutterstock Images/newcorner; p. 77 (TL): Alamy/©Dmitriy Shironosov; p. 77 (TC): Alamy/©Chris Ryan/OJO Images Ltd; p. 77 (TL): Alamy/©Bubbles Photolibrary; p. 77 (CL): Alamy/©Greg Balfour Evans; p. 77 (C): Alamy/©DreamPictures/Blend Images; p. 77 (CR): Superstock; p. 77 (BR): Alamy/©Myrleen Pearson; p. 77 (BCR): Alamy/©Frederic Cirou/ PhotoAlto; p. 77 (BCL): Alamy/©Pablo Paul; p. 77 (BL): Alamy/©Tetra Images; p. 81 (TL): Alamy/©Philimages; p. 81 (C): Alamy/©Imran Ahmed; p. 81 (CL): Alamy/©fenghuai dong; p. 81 (B): Alamy/©John Crowe; p.82 (T): Shutterstock Images/magicinfoto; p.85 (TL): Shutterstock Images/ lornet; p.87 (CL): Alamy/©Helene Rogers/Art Directors & TRIP; p.88 (TL): Alamy/©Patricia Phillips; p. 88 (TR): Shutterstock Images/Africa Studio; p.88 (BR): Shutterstock Images/soloir; p.88 (BL): Shutterstock Images/A and N photography; p.89 (CR): Shutterstock Images/prudkov.

The publishers are grateful to the following illustrators:

David Belmonte (Beehive Illustration) p. 28, 30; Alberto de Hoyos: p. 17, 24, 34, 67, 75, 79; Nigel Dobbyn p. 19; Mark Draisey p. 25; Mark Duffin p. 4, 47, 49, 64; emc p. 14; Jose Rubio p. 5; David Shephard: p. 4, 27, 74; Norbert Sipos (Beehive Illustration) p. 17, 39, 48, 59, 64, 69, 70; Sean Tiffany p. 24, 50, 80.

CAMBRIDGE
UNIVERSITY PRESS

University Printing House, Cambridge CB2 8BS, United Kingdom

One Liberty Plaza, 20th Floor, New York, NY 10006, USA

477 Williamstown Road, Port Melbourne, VIC 3207, Australia

4843/24, 2nd Floor, Ansari Road, Daryaganj, Delhi – 110002, India

79 Anson Road, #06–04/06, Singapore 079906

Cambridge University Press is part of the University of Cambridge.

It furthers the University's mission by disseminating knowledge in the pursuit of education, learning and research at the highest international levels of excellence.

www.cambridge.org
Information on this title: www.cambridge.org/9781107488182

First published 2015
20 19 18 17 16 15 14 13 12 11 10 9 8 7

Printed by Vivar Printing, Malaysia

A catalogue record for this publication is available from the British Library

ISBN 978-1-107-46749-1 Student's Book with Online Workbook and Online Practice
ISBN 978-1-107-46744-6 Student's Book
ISBN 978-1-107-46750-7 Workbook with Online Practice
ISBN 978-1-107-48818-2 Combo A with Online Workbook and Online Practice
ISBN 978-1-107-48820-5 Combo B with Online Workbook and Online Practice
ISBN 978-1-107-46755-2 Teacher's Book
ISBN 978-1-107-46759-0 Audio CDs (3)
ISBN 978-1-107-46761-3 Video DVD
ISBN 978-1-107-48823-6 Presentation Plus DVD-ROM

Additional resources for this publication at www.cambridgelms.org/eyesopen

This book contains the first half of the complete edition of *Eyes Open* Student's Book 2 and Workbook 2. Please note that the page numbers are the same as the complete Student's Book and Workbook.